T0274268

"Annie Dillard memorably wrote, 'How we spend our days is, of course, how we spend our lives.' There is only the particular. And the Christian faith gives us a distinct place to stand in the present, formed by a specific history and drawn by the eschatological Spirit into God's future. Yet, as James Smith shows, often proponents of the very faith, which should locate us most clearly in God's time, settle for the parody—'nowhen' Christians. This book has helped me—genuinely. James Smith has helped me think about the subject of time in a fresh way. I greatly enjoyed the distilled wisdom, the broad philosophical engagement, the connecting of Scripture, tradition, and culture. Truly this book is a gift which has engaged my awareness of how we are called to live the gifts which are our lives. My hope and prayer is that the impact of this book on how we live—on the times of our lives—will be exponentially more than the time it took to read it."

—**The Most Rev. Justin Welby**, Archbishop of Canterbury

"'A life is always a life*time*, and ours is a time of toil,' writes James K. A. Smith. But he shows us that time is more than toil. It is a gift waiting to be redeemed, and a central conviction of this book is that 'the Lord of the star fields' is intimately attuned to our haunted, beautiful histories. Dwelling with these lucid, winsome meditations on 'spiritual timekeeping' was like listening in on a lively conversation between St. Augustine, Gustavo Gutiérrez, James Baldwin, and Marilynne Robinson, while Pink Floyd's *Dark Side of the Moon* played in the background."

—**Fred Bahnson**, author of *Soil and Sacrament*

# HOW TO INHABIT TIME

# HOW TO INHABIT TIME

## UNDERSTANDING THE PAST, FACING THE FUTURE, LIVING FAITHFULLY NOW

• • •

JAMES K. A. SMITH

BrazosPress
a division of Baker Publishing Group
Grand Rapids, Michigan

Published by Brazos Press
a division of Baker Publishing Group
PO Box 6287, Grand Rapids, MI 49516-6287
www.brazospress.com

Printed in the United States of America



Library of Congress Cataloging-in-Publication Data
Names: Smith, James K. A., 1970– author.
Title: How to inhabit time : understanding the past, facing the future, living faithfully now / James K.A. Smith.
Description: Grand Rapids, Michigan : Brazos Press, a division of Baker Publishing Group, [2022] | Includes bibliographical references.
Identifiers: LCCN 2022009317 | ISBN 9781587435232 (cloth) | ISBN 9781587435911 (ITPE) | ISBN 9781493438624 (ebook) | ISBN 9781493438631 (pdf)
Subjects: LCSH: Time—Biblical teaching. | Bible. Ecclesiastes, III—Criticism, interpretation, etc. | Time—Religious aspects—Christianity.
Classification: LCC BS1475.6.T5 S65 2022 | DDC 223/.806—dc23/eng/20220321
LC record available at https://lccn.loc.gov/2022009317



Baker Publishing Group publications use paper produced from sustainable forestry practices and post-consumer waste whenever possible.

22 23 24 25 26 27 28    7 6 5 4 3 2 1

For

**Sue Johnson**

*in memoriam*

You always had time for us;
we had too little with you.

To hope in Christ is at the same time to believe in the adventure of history.

—Gustavo Gutiérrez, *A Theology of Liberation*

I am sittin' among you to watch; and every once and a while I will come out and tell you what time of night it is.

—Sojourner Truth

Christians have no right to be ignorant of history just because they stand in the truth.

—Calvin Seerveld, *Rainbows for the Fallen World*

The absolute is available to everyone in every age. There never was a more holy age than ours, and never a less.

—Annie Dillard, *For the Time Being*

So much of the trouble of this world is caused by memories, for we only remember half.

—Apsley Cherry-Garrard, *The Worst Journey in the World*

All that can save you now is your confrontation with your own history . . . which is not your past, but your present.

—James Baldwin

We ought not to want to live ahead of time with only the saints and righteous.

—Augustine, Letter 189

# CONTENTS

# PREFACE

This book is an invitation to the spiritual adventure we call "time." If it promises guidance on how to inhabit time, please don't expect formulas or methods or tips for managing your day planner. Instead, the hope of this book is to occasion an awakening, a dawning awareness of what it means to be the sorts of creatures who dwell in the flux of time's flow, who swim in the river of history. Knowing *when* we are can change everything. Knowing whether it's dawn or dusk changes how you live the next moment.

The aim of this book is to encourage a sort of *recognition* that is the fruit of *contemplation*. We emerge from the hard, quiet work of contemplation with a new recognition of ourselves, our world, and our relation to the God who encounters us in the fullness of time. As the philosopher Charles Taylor puts it, to recognize one's connection with the Spirit in history is "to change oneself and the way one acts."[1] It's like living amid the cacophony of the modern world and finally discerning the beat of the Spirit in history and knowing how to dance in time.

But recognition of the Spirit's drumbeat requires careful attention, pausing to become attuned to the world in a new way. Such discernment is the fruit of reflection, rumination, contemplation. This book, you might say, is an exercise in such attunement, an invitation to ruminate on questions we perhaps haven't asked. The wager is that such reflection, as Taylor says, changes us and thus changes how we live, even if I can't prescribe exactly what it looks like for you to answer the Spirit's call on your life.

You can feel this connection between contemplation and action, reflection and transformation, in Rainer Maria Rilke's poem "Archaic Torso of Apollo." The poet encounters the truncated beauty of an ancient statue that, even without the glare of eyes, makes him feel seen. Standing mesmerized before the stone that seems alive, the narrator beholds himself anew. The encounter is a recognition that yields the stark conclusion of the poem: "You must change your life."[2]

This book hopes for such self-recognition. But this recognition is more like an awareness that dawns than an argument that can be grasped or a formula that can be repeated. A word of encouragement before you enter: don't come so much to learn as to *dwell*. This book is something other than a package of information between two covers. We will begin to understand our place and calling in the spiritual adventure of history only if we find a way to hit the pause button on our frenetic absorption in the everyday and resist the tyranny of the urgent. That's precisely why this book is a blend of philosophy and poetry, memoir and theology.

Reflection is hard, especially in a culture bent on distraction and superficiality. If this book offers some philosophers as guides for such an undertaking, that's only because philosophy is a perennial invitation to reflect on how we live—to cultivate an "examined life," as Socrates put it. I hope this book revives the ancient art of philosophy as spiritual counsel. Philosophy matters only if it teaches us how to live, how to be human. The philosophers you'll meet in the pages that follow are catalysts for such reflection. Don't worry if philosophy doesn't come easily to you. The difficulty is the point ("a feature, not a bug," as they say). Sometimes we need the difficulty to get us to slow down and look at ourselves.

Slowing down is how we learn to notice what we usually speed past. So just as crucial to the spiritual exercise of this book is an array of images and anecdotes, portraits of time from nature, art, and history, some drawn from my own story, all of which are invitations to reflect on what's right in front of us yet so often invisible. Imagine this book as an impressionist painting of sorts. The point isn't to "picture reality" by transcribing it; the point is to transform our *attention* to reality by reframing our focus. The pictures and poems and images are not detours or distractions or "illustrations." Don't rush to get through them in order to get to "the point." Taking time to dwell with the images *is* the point. Taking the time to enjoy reading and to revel in language is one of the ways we learn to inhabit time well.

Thus begins our adventure of reckoning, discernment, and hope.

# INTRODUCTION

## *When Are We?*
## *The Spiritual Significance of Timekeeping*

> That which is, already has been; that which is to be, already is; and God seeks out what has gone by.
>
> —Ecclesiastes 3:15

When I didn't know where else to turn; when the cloud of depression had enveloped me and my loved ones; when all I seemed to do was rage, my shouts like some misguided attempt at sonar location from the fog; when the thoughts of ending it all became too frequent—then, finally, humbled if not humiliated, I entered the counselor's office. I didn't even know what to ask.

I recall an early exercise. "Draw me a map of your childhood house," he suggested. With years of hindsight now, I can see this was an invitation to orient myself, to get my bearings. I came in lost, disoriented, and the mapping exercise was an invitation for me, blind, to reach out my hands and feel my way to some landmarks, the way you feel your way through a house in the dark.

What he couldn't have known was how many years of my childhood I had dreamed of being an architect. Just picking up a pencil to draw brought back a rush of muscle memories. My high school drafting classes came back to my hand like riding a bike. I remembered instantly how to mark the doors and windows, even how to do those perfect, simple arrowheads that mark dimensions. I'm gaining control, confidence. I'm thinking, "I've been here before."

But my soul is now back in that split-level home on Snakes Trail Road where our family fell apart. Here's the massive garage where my father built his hot rods and repaired snowmobiles. Down the stairs, in the basement, wood-paneled with a tiny window, is the room where I felt terrified by my father when I was eleven. In the rec room, near the bar and the hi-fi with its 8-tracks, is the blue flowered couch where our parents told us it was over and that we—my mother, brother, and I—would be leaving. Upstairs are the two bedrooms that used to be ours but are now occupied by his mistress's children, all signs of our being there erased.

"All houses have memory," writes David Farrier. "Every house is a clock."[1] I'm drawing a map but inhabiting a history. This looks like cartography but is actually archaeology. If every house is a clock, this floor plan is a timeline. This isn't a structure "out there" on a dirt road in southern Ontario, this is the house in me. This isn't a clock I carry in my pocket, but more like a time bomb that's been tick, tick, ticking in my soul for thirty years.

I can draw this house with my eyes closed. I am mapping every windowsill, picturing closets, placing the furniture, recalling the way light settled on the sunken living room. My map ventures outside to the yard: here's the sandbox by the garden that spills onto the massive hill that was a dream for our toboggans. There's the path along the cornfield to the woods where we spent countless hours building forts. There's Mud Creek, with that curious bit of sandy "beach" where my friends and I talked about which of Charlie's Angels was most beautiful. This is a map of the field of dreams that was my childhood until it wasn't.

• • •

We usually think of disorientation as a matter of being displaced, a confusion about *where* one is. You know the clichéd film scene: someone awakes from a trauma and asks, "Where am I?" But disorientation can be temporal too. When "time is out of joint," as Hamlet put it, we are dislocated. You awake some morning in a strange haze of barely awareness, and it takes several beats to remember what day it is. Depending on how many beats intervene, anxiety arises from a temporal vertigo. There are many ways to be disoriented by time, like the glitch of déjà vu or the time warp of going home again. Sometimes we default to a spatial question for what is, at root, temporal disorientation. When I experience that early morning temporal fog, I might be asking myself, "Where am I?" even if the unvoiced question, though grammatically strange, should be, "*When* am I?"

Now consider a different kind of disorientation: someone who doesn't even realize they're lost because they are so confident they know where they are, like the stereotypical dad who blithely forges on in the wrong direction, more confident in his sense of direction than the road atlas in his wife's hands. Or, more terrifying, the image of Lieutenant Dike in *Band of Brothers*, whose misplaced confidence in his sense of orientation leads to senseless death. This disorientation stems from a delusion, whether of naivete or hubris, of imagining they are above it all, and especially above correction.

There is a kind of *temporal* dislocation akin to such unrecognized disorientation. I'm thinking of a kind of temporal disorientation that is unrecognized because it's buried and hidden by the illusion of being above the fray, immune to history, surfing time rather than being immersed and battered by its waves. Such temporal disorientation stems from the delusion of being "nowhen," unconditioned by time.[2] Those who imagine they inhabit nowhen imagine themselves wholly governed by timeless principles, unchanging convictions, expressing an idealism that assumes they are wholly governed by eternal ideas untainted by history. They are oblivious to the deposits of history in their own unconscious. They have never considered the archaeological strata in their own souls. They live as if hatched rather than born, created ex nihilo rather than formed by a process. They don't realize that the homes that formed them were clocks. They can't hear the ticking. Where such an eternal nowhen rules, time doesn't matter.

This temporal delusion characterizes too much of Christianity and too many Christians (and not a few Americans).

• • •

When the human cerebellum is injured or ill, whether through trauma or disease or genetic inheritance, a curious condition can arise: *dyschronometria*, an inability to keep time. Lacking a reliable internal clock, the person suffering from dyschronometria becomes lost in a temporal fog. They lack any sense of the passage of time, the psychological tick-tock that guides us in a day. A minute feels the same as an hour; hours bleed into a blur.

This distorted time perception can go unnoticed, yet be dangerous and debilitating. For example, a person suffering from dementia who manifests dyschronometria will have no awareness of having already taken their pills and thus take them again. Or a parent who has suffered brain trauma may lose track of time, become derailed and disoriented, and constantly struggle to remember to pick up children from school. For someone suffering from dyschronometria, their temporal life has no texture. Like a flat winter plain under cloudy skies, time is an expanse without ripple or shadow. Nothing is distinct.

A lot of contemporary Christianity suffers from spiritual dyschronometria—an inability to keep time, a lack of awareness of what time it is. Too many contemporary Christians look at history and see only a barren, textureless landscape. We might think of this as the temporal equivalent of color blindness—a failure to appreciate the nuances and dynamics of history. We can't discern why *when* makes a difference. We don't recognize how much we are the products of a past, leading to naivete about our present. But we also don't know how to keep time with a promised future, leading to fixations on the "end times" rather than cultivating a posture of hope.

This temporal tone deafness is a feature of the view from nowhen that characterizes too much of contemporary Christianity. We think biblical ideas are timeless formulas to be instituted anywhere and everywhere in the same way. While we rightly entrust ourselves to a God who is the same today, yesterday, and forever, we mistakenly imagine this translates into a one-size-fits-all approach to what faithfulness looks like. We are blind to our own locatedness, geographically, historically, temporally. Even expressions of Christianity that seem to be fixated on time and history are, ironically, nowhen renditions of the faith that believe they are above time and history because they've been granted access to a God's-eye view of it all.

When I first became a Christian in my late teens, my entrée to the faith was through a sect that invented what we now call "dispensationalism"—a way of reading the Bible, spawned in the nineteenth century, that is fixated on reading history in light of the end times. John Nelson Darby, Charles Scofield, and others discerned epochs or "dispensations" of history in their curious (and innovative) reading of the Bible that had everyone looking for the rapture, worried about being left behind. As an eager student of the Bible, I drank up this esoteric insider knowledge of both history and the future. All of it was embodied, for me, in a visual aid that dominated the basement of that tiny chapel in Tavistock, Ontario. Hovering over every Bible study was a massive, wall-sized version of one of Clarence Larkin's famous charts that mapped the sweep of human history (a whole "7,000 years" according to Larkin) while also mapping out what was to come.

Like a schematic diagram of the history of creation, Larkin charts the dramatic sweep of time between the parentheses of two eternities. Almost the entirety of history is assigned to a long era of degeneration. What the future holds is an escape from time. The rest is countdown. (At the time of my conversion, a tract was making its rounds spelling out "88 Reasons for 1988.")

On the one hand, this *looks* like a form of Christianity that is fascinated by history. But, in fact, the charts and predictions manifest a Christianity that believes it is *above* history. History is the regrettable grind of waiting, the churn of degeneration, the countdown of demise. Long chunks of history, including a long phase of Christianity between the death of the apostles and the momentous 1928 insights of John Nelson Darby, are devoid of the Spirit, eras of disillusion, superstition, and deception. Instead of discerning history, dispensationalism is a nowhen Christianity that mostly demonizes history.

Despite pretending to prioritize faithfulness, the spiritual dyschronometria of nowhen Christianities actually generates *un*faithful responses to the present. Let's take just one glaring example. In the wake of systemic police brutality disproportionately inflicted on Black Americans, a movement swelled to rightly assert that "Black Lives Matter." The assertion was necessary because of a distinct and particular history of oppression and exploitation, a history that was far from past. In the face of this, a number of white Christians were suddenly surprising purveyors of a universal human solidarity and, against the supposedly selective or narrow protest that "Black Lives Matter," asserted that "All Lives Matter." Apart from the rather selective attention to such universal principles, those who asserted that "All Lives Matter" took themselves to be articulating an eternal idea and ideal.

But the question isn't simply what's true; the question is what needs to be said and done *now*, in this place and in this moment given this particular history. To assert that "All Lives Matter" as a response to "Black Lives Matter" is not wrong in principle but *temporally*. It fails to recognize that "Black Lives Matter" is something that has to be said here *and now* because of a specific (contingent) history that got us here. The assertion of the ideal, timeless truth that "All Lives Matter" is performatively false in such a situation. It lacks prudence and does not constitute faithful witness here, in *this* now. Our (shared) history makes all the difference for discerning what faithfulness looks like.[3]

This is just one example of the collective—social and political—implications of a properly *temporal* spirituality. There are also implications for personal discipleship. For example, nowhen Christianities that treat time as flat lack the pastoral subtlety and nuance to minister to people in different seasons of life. Whether in my own spiritual life or, say, the lifelong journey of a marriage, recognizing the reality of *seasons* can be incredibly liberating, not only because it changes our expectations but also because it attunes us to receive God's grace in different ways in different eras of a life. The spiritual dynamics of time and history are at once communal and individual, personal and political. We must attend to *our* history just as I face my own. Reckoning and hope scale to both soul and society.

• • •

What we need to counter spiritual dyschronometria and the fiction of nowhen Christianities is a renewed temporal awareness, a spiritual timekeeping that is attuned to the texture of history, the vicissitudes of life, and the tempo of the Spirit.

Such spiritual timekeeping isn't just counting, like ticks on the clock or crossing out days on the calendar. To "number our days" (Ps. 90:12) is not just to count down, making notches on the wall as we hurtle toward the day we can't count. Rather, this is counsel to know when we are, to find our bearings by an orientation to time and history. We are mortal, not just because we die but because we are the sorts of creatures whose very being is lived in time. Being mortal means being temporal.

Spiritual timekeeping is fundamentally a matter of awakening to our embeddedness in history and attending to our temporality—both individually and collectively. It is an exercise in drawing the map of the houses that built us. This is less a matter of sorting out the mysteries of what time *is* and more importantly discerning how time shapes us, as both history and future. "I confess to you, Lord, that I still do not know what time is," Augustine admitted, "and I further confess to you, Lord, that as I say this I know myself to be conditioned by time."[4] It is this *conditioning* that nowhen Christianities refuse to recognize; it is the spiritual significance of such conditioning that interests us here.

As a creature, every disciple is a temporal being, and our embeddedness in time and history is crucial for discerning what the shape of faithfulness looks like. We, both individually and collectively, are products of a contingent history. Our identities are bound up with roads taken and not. Like trees whose rings tell the story of fires and droughts from a distant past, our character and capacities reflect histories that long preceded us as well as the personal histories that amount to our own story. A faithful Christian life is a matter of keeping time with the Spirit. But what the Spirit asks of us always reflects history—our own, but also the history of the church and the societies in which we find ourselves. "What do we do *now*?" is one of the fundamental questions of discipleship.

We are not just talking about what to do spiritually with your time, as if time were one more commodity to spend wisely. The book of hours, for instance, is an ancient devotional device, and the liturgical calendar is an important collective discipline for the church. But what you hold in your hands is not a book about praying the hours or, God forbid, spiritualizing time management. This book is intended as a wake-up call to the significance of your temporality, *our* temporality—awakening to the way history lives in you, the way we inhabit history and history inhabits us, and the way futurity pulls us and shapes us. It's not as simple as seeing the spiritual significance of your calendar but instead discerning the spiritual repercussions of a history that precedes you, lives in you, and shapes the future to which you are called.

Facing up to the spiritual significance of time, history, and futurity is almost the exact opposite of "management"; it is more like voluntary exposure to disruption, making oneself vulnerable to haunting. To face the spiritual significance of history is to contend with ghosts. We don't need coaches who will help us manage our time; we need prophets who make us face our histories (and futures). No one knew the spiritual significance of such historical reckoning better than James Baldwin. In a jarring essay he wrote for *Ebony* magazine in 1965, Baldwin named this:

> White man, hear me! History, as nearly no one seems to know, is not merely something to be read. And it does not refer merely, or even principally, to the past. On the contrary, the great force of history comes from the fact that we carry it within us. . . . And it is with great pain and terror that one begins to realize this. . . . In great pain and terror because . . . one enters into battle with that historical creation, Oneself, and attempts to recreate oneself according to a principle more humane and more liberating.[5]

What Baldwin says about our collective history is equally true of our personal histories. That map I drew in the counselor's office was the beginning of painful labor, the work I had to do confronting Myself, the "Oneself" produced by that place and, more significantly, by my time in that place. My "I" is a "historical creation," as Baldwin puts it, with strata of sediment, layers of formation, the charred lines of trauma in my history. I won't know who I am until I know *when* I am. But the heartbreaking labor of that confrontation is also a beginning, a liberation, as Baldwin puts it, opening up a new future.

The miracle of grace, Jesus said, is that we could be "born again" (John 3.3). Part of what makes this miraculous is that the new birth is not a blank slate. Nicodemus doesn't understand this. He can only imagine being born again by rewinding the clock ("Can one enter a second time into the mother's womb and be born?" John 3:4). Jesus is inviting him to consider the unthinkable: that this *I*, this historical creation, can be born again, can begin again. And not because God erases history;

that would mean erasing me, this "I" that is a historical creation. The miracle that puzzled Nicodemus, that should astound us, is that the God of grace can redeem even me—this historical creation—can begin again with this history that lives in me, that *is* me. It's the body with scars that is resurrected; it's the me with a history that is redeemed, forgiven, graced, liberated.

And *we* with our history need to do the same work of spiritually confronting the Ourself that has been created by the contingencies, choices, and injustices of history if a different future is going to be possible. Pick your "we": it might be a congregation, a neighborhood, an institution; it might be the larger collectives of the church, a society, a nation. Baldwin's insight holds true: all of these collectives are historical creations, and if the future is going to be different—if grace is going to reach these behemoths of history—the painful labor of confronting that history is the only way to give birth to a different future. This isn't a matter of antiquarian fascination, like a hobby-historian's interest in World War II programs on the History Channel; this is a matter of life and death in the present. It's not a question of our past but a matter of who we *are* and *will be*. Again, Baldwin names this necessity:

> All that can save you now is your confrontation with your own history . . . which is not your past, but your present. Nobody cares what happened in the past. One can't afford to care what happened in the past. But your history has led you to this moment, and you can only begin to change yourself and save yourself by looking at what you are doing in the name of your history.[6]

Now, I'm not sure that even such confrontation with history means we can "save" ourselves, as Baldwin says. But if we are going to be saved, we will certainly need to work out our salvation with fear and trembling as we come to terms with our histories.

• • •

The work of spiritual confrontation with our histories is a crucial part—though only a part—of the sort of disciplined temporal awareness I'm calling "spiritual timekeeping." The prescription for our dyschronometria is a renewed time consciousness, a mindful regard for history, a dawning awareness of what it means to be a creature *of* and *in* the flow of time, with the accretions of history and the incessant waves that press us toward the shore of the future.

We might imagine spiritual timekeeping as an expansion of the spiritual discipline of *memento mori*, the disciplined habit of keeping death before us. Christians appropriated this practice of the Stoics with the inflection of the Psalms and the scent of ash. Thus St. Benedict counsels in his Rule: "Keep death daily before your eyes."[7]

The Baroque Flemish painter Philippe de Champaigne (whose painting of St. Augustine hangs in the Los Angeles County Museum of Art) painted a famous seventeenth-century invocation of this Benedictine counsel called, simply, *Vanité*, often known in English as "Still Life with a Skull." The image is something of a triptych: the jarring, hollow glare of a skull is flanked by the bright life of a tulip on the left, already picked and thus dying, and an hourglass on the right, whose time is passing. Number thy days. Keep death before you.

In the spirit of *memento mori*, consider this book an invitation to the discipline of what we might call *memento tempori*. Remember you are temporal. Keep your history daily before you. Remember there is a future after the sand runs out, and that future is already bleeding into your present. *Dum spiro spero*: while I breathe, I hope.

Such temporal awareness must be cultivated. Like a child who climbs the tree in the field and finds the horizon widening, their world expanding, so a renewed time consciousness transforms our sense of place in God's story—what German theologians, in a wonderful word you can sort of chew on, liked to call *Heilsgeschichte*, "holy history," the unfurling of history as the drama of salvation. Each chapter of this book is an exercise in cultivating temporal awareness, a new angle on the ways the Spirit courses through time.

• • •

We need to remember that at the heart of Christianity is not a teaching or a message or even a doctrine but an *event*. God's self-revelation unfolds in time, and redemption is accomplished by what *happens*.

This truth is something that philosophers, more than theologians, have impressed upon me. It was perhaps the Danish philosopher Søren Kierkegaard who was the first catalyst in this regard. In his short work *Philosophical Fragments*, Kierkegaard works out why Christianity accords a unique significance to time. He contrasts a Christian understanding of time with what he calls the Socratic model, after Plato's teacher. Socrates, we might say, was a proponent of a view from nowhen, an idealist conception of time in which, really, at the end of the day, time doesn't matter. What *happens* doesn't really change anything, for Socrates. Even when I become "enlightened," when I come to know the truth, he says, I'm only recollecting what I already knew. Time doesn't really make a difference. Indeed, the goal is to somehow *overcome* time to get to eternity.

In contrast, Kierkegaard says, in the Christian understanding of time, the instant of revelation—and the instant in which I am confronted by such revelation—is a decisive "moment" that changes everything. Things *change* in time, and that change is momentous—an emigration from darkness to light (Eph. 5:8), from death to life (Eph. 2:4–5), from nonbeing to being (1 Cor. 1:28). The moment is charged and pregnant, a turning point for the cosmos. History matters. What happens makes a difference. When I, at some point in time, am confronted with the mystery that the eternal God became human in the fullness of time, "then the moment in time must have such decisive significance that for no moment will I be able to forget it, neither in time nor in eternity, because the eternal, previously nonexistent, came into existence in that moment."[8] Time and history are not just pseudostages on which to roll out timeless truths, like some mock unveiling of an open secret; rather, the truth is born at the very intersection of time and eternity, like a chemical reaction that requires both components. It might take only an instant, "the blink of an eye," and yet it is the *happening* that makes all the difference. "A moment such as this is unique," Kierkegaard continues. "To be sure, it is short and temporal, as the moment is; it is passing, as the moment is, past, as the moment is in the next moment, and yet it is decisive, and yet it is filled with the eternal. A moment such as this must have a special name. Let us call it: *the fullness of time*."[9] The paradigm of this intersection of time and eternity is the incarnation of God in Christ—the moment that is the fulcrum of human history. The intersection of time and eternity makes a difference for both. In history we see the contrails of the Spirit's movement.

One of my favorite twentieth-century philosophers, O. K. Bouwsma, was deeply influenced by Kierkegaard. You can sense that influence in a succinct and beautiful passage in which Bouwsma emphasizes "that Christianity is something that happened, and not a theory or an explanation or a set of doctrines." Because Christianity is fundamentally a "happening," we rightly understand it only in terms of story.

> We all know that the story to which I have now referred is a long, long story and that the happening is a long, long happening. The happening takes place over many centuries, the story is composed of innumerable episodes—a story that is continued in sequels indefinitely.[10]

In fact, Bouwsma argues, we need to understand this story as a "love story" in which the Christian "becomes a character in the as-yet-unwritten continuation of the story" insofar as they come to see the story as a story about themselves, a story that transforms them not least by transforming their self-understanding.[11] To be(come) a Christian is to live into this happening.

In 1927 a young, as-yet-unknown German philosopher named Martin Heidegger, a student of Kierkegaard, gave a lecture to the theologians at the university in Marburg.[12] Musing on the nature and calling of theology, Heidegger emphasized, shockingly, that theology's "topic" was not God but instead what he called *Christlichkeit*—"Christianness," or the *how* of Christian existence. Theology, he emphasized, should reflect the very nature of faith, which is "not some more or less modified type of knowing" but rather a faith-full way of being in response to the event of revelation in "Christ, the crucified God." Faith is a *how* and, more specifically, a way of living in light of an *event*. Faith—the existential transformation called "rebirth"—is a mode of participating in the Christ-*event*. Because of this, Heidegger doesn't talk about "Christianity" as an abstraction or something merely to be believed. Instead, he speaks of "the Christian occurrence"—the Christ-*happening*.

Being a Christian, then, is not so much a matter of believing something about God as much as living in light of this event's cascading effects on history. Christian faith is ongoing participation in the Christ-event which continues to rumble through human history. Christianity is less a *what* and more a *how*, a question of how to live given what has happened in Christ.

Thus Heidegger offers a unique definition of "faith." His language is technical and a bit laborious, but I think it's worth pausing to reflect on it and unpack the implications for faithfulness in time. "Faith," he says, is "*the believing-understanding mode of existing in the history revealed, i.e., occurring, with the Crucified.*" The radicality of Heidegger's argument is sort of buried in the prepositions here. Faith, he's saying, is a *how*, a way of being, a "form of life" that is primarily a call to live "in" the historical event of the Crucified—the life, death, resurrection, and ascension of the incarnate God. To live "in" that historical event is to live "with" the Crucified. Living into this event is fundamentally about communion with the crucified God. Whatever else we might say about it, the Christian life is a way of life that lives as if this history still matters—to live as if this history is now, and that this history is *my* history.[13]

Living "into" the history of revelation—living into the historical occurrence of the crucified God—is the call of the Christian life. But that requires a kind of historical consciousness that is eviscerated by too many forms of Christianity that amount to systematic forgetting.

• • •

What I'm calling the art of spiritual timekeeping—living out the faith with a disciplined temporal awareness—is informed by four fundamental convictions. First, spiritual timekeeping is the working out of our creaturely finitude as creatures embedded in time (what Augustine described as our being "conditioned by time").[14] For every creature, to be is to become; to exist is to change; to have and to hold is to lose and to mourn; to awake is to hope. The baby's chubby wrinkles presage the elder's craggy folds. Autumn's fire is latent in spring's green. What difference does this make for living a life, as creatures, in communion with an eternal God? What this means for faith across a lifetime of becoming is at the heart of spiritual timekeeping, and we will explore different facets of this in the chapters below: how to forget, how to remember; how to mourn, how to enjoy what's fleeting; how to wait, how to hope.

Second, spiritual timekeeping reflects a sense of time shaped by covenant—a promise made in history reverberates through subsequent time. God's covenant with Abraham is the paradigm, finding its culmination in Jesus's incarnational promise to never leave us or forsake us, even "to the very end of the age" (Matt. 28:20 NIV). That is a promise of presence *through* history—not above it or in spite of it. The promise itself recognizes our immersion in history, our subjection to the ages. As Annie Dillard once observed, "The absolute is available to everyone in every age. There never was a more holy age than ours, and never a less."[15]

Third, spiritual timekeeping is nourished by Jesus's promise that the Spirit will guide us into all truth across time (John 16:13). This stands in contrast to what I'll call the "primitivism" of so much American Christianity. Primitivism is a curious view of history that sees God's presence limited to only key points in history. Most importantly, primitivist Christianities assume that the Spirit was present in the first century and then somehow absent and forgotten for the long intervening centuries until someone (usually the leader of *their* sect) rediscovered "the truth" in the nineteenth century, say, and spawned a "renewal" movement that "recovered" the original, primitive truth. Such primitivism writes off vast swaths of history as "Ichabod,"[16] devoid of God's presence, because that history doesn't conform to their contemporary version of the original. In contrast, Jesus promises a dynamic work of the Spirit, who guides us into truth across time. This is the fundamental conviction of *catholicity*: the Spirit continues to guide and lead into the future, across history, still guiding, convicting, illuminating, and revealing, which is precisely why ongoing reform is necessary. The story is still unfolding. Listening to the Spirit is not an archaeological dig for some original deposit but rather an attunement to a God *with* us, still speaking, still surprising, still revealing.

Finally, spiritual timekeeping is animated by the future. Such a futural orientation we call "hope." The church is a people of the future, a kingdom-come community that is always learning anew how to wait. The popular fixation on the end times is actually fundamentally ahistorical: it sees the present as merely a countdown to what is dictated by some supposed future that has already been determined, with charts to diagram the sequence. Such end-times eschatologies are just chronological countdowns to an end. But apocalyptic literature in the Bible is interested not in *chronos* ("clock time," as Heidegger calls it) but in *kairos*, a fullness of time, a time charged in a way that can't be simply measured. Christian eschatological hope is a *kairological* orientation to an inbreaking future that makes an impact on our present. The end-times countdown is a decline narrative: the clock is ticking to the rapture; everything in the meantime is just time endured before the escape pod descends. In contrast, spiritual timekeeping tries to discern where the Spirit's restoration is already afoot in creation's groaning.

These four theological convictions inform spiritual timekeeping. They are revelational realities that tune the clock of a spiritually sensitive people of God. And such attunement happens less through doctrinal treatises and more through the spiritual disciplines of the church's worship, reflecting the liturgical calendar, which, as we'll see in chapter 3 below, reflects the way sacred time "bends." Like the map we carry in our hearts, the church's practices are disciplines of attunement that calibrate the spiritual timekeeping we carry in our bones. The habits of *memento tempori* are formed by the church's practices of disciplined temporal awareness. What we need is not sensationalist end-times countdowns but a practical eschatology that enables us to live as a futural people animated by hope.

In nowhen forms of Christianity, the watchword is "preservation"; faithfulness is understood as the prolongation and preservation of what has been (often oblivious to how recent their version of "the fundamentals" is). In other words, in nowhen Christianity, faithfulness is a matter of guarding against change. In spiritual timekeeping, the watchword is "discernment"; faithfulness requires knowing when we are in order to discern what we are called to. In nowhen forms of Christianity, faithfulness is equated with sustaining a stasis; spiritual timekeeping, in contrast, is characterized by a dynamism of keeping time with the Spirit.

Keeping time with the Spirit is less a regimental march—*left, right, left, right!* ad infinitum—and more like a subtle dance, a responsive feel for what comes next. Lionel Salter offers a parallel in his description of a conductor's role in an orchestra. "The conductor has to judge the proper *tempo* of the work, and indicate it clearly to the orchestra by movements of his baton." But this is not just a mechanical process. What the music requires of the orchestra changes over the course of a symphony. If tempo were just a mechanical factor of timekeeping, "it would be sufficient to play the orchestra a couple of ticks from a metronome, or, as sometimes in dance bands, say 'One—two,' to set the right tempo for the whole piece." But of course that's *not* what happens with an orchestra, because playing the symphony well requires different timing across the course of the work. "One of the beauties of music," Salter remarks, "lies in its subtle variations of pace—the urging on, the yielding, the big broadening." The conductor is helping the entire orchestra to become attuned to these subtleties.[17]

So, too, must the church be attuned to the living Spirit's "conducting" in ways that are responsive to the moment: when to urge on, when to yield. Such discernment is true for the collective body of Christ in its communal witness and mission. But these dynamics of time are also important for one's own spiritual life: to recognize, for example, seasons of a life with God, when the Spirit sometimes speaks *sotto voce*, almost inaudibly, and to discern what God asks of us in such a season—what God is doing *in* us in such a season. Hence, the wisdom and discernment of spiritual timekeeping is integral to a life well-lived.

This book aims to help Christians know what time it is. I hope it might be an exercise akin to what my counselor asked of me, a discipline that Baldwin said is required of us: an exercise of reckoning with the histories we carry, an archaeology of our wounds and hopes, the way our home-clocks wound us in a particular way—and what God asks of us in our singular, pregnant *now*.

## MEDITATION 1

# ECCLESIASTES 3:9–15 (NIV)

[9] What do workers gain from their toil? [10] I have seen the burden God has laid on the human race. [11] He has made everything beautiful in its time. He has also set eternity in the human heart; yet no one can fathom what God has done from beginning to end. [12] I know that there is nothing better for people than to be happy and to do good while they live. [13] That each of them may eat and drink, and find satisfaction in all their toil—this is the gift of God. [14] I know that everything God does will endure forever; nothing can be added to it and nothing taken from it. God does it so that people will fear him.

[15] Whatever is has already been,
and what will be has been before;
and God will call the past to account.

Toil and time. These are the warp and woof of our existence in this clear-eyed appraisal of the human condition. Each is a constant companion of our sojourn. A life is always a life*time*, and ours is a time of toil. But both seem preferable to the alternative; to escape toil would mean evading time. To evade time would mean ceasing to be. So maybe time is a gift? Maybe even the toil is a gift?

This passage, like the whole of Ecclesiastes, evinces a profound ambivalence. You can feel translators wrestling with this ambiguity. Perhaps the ambiguity exists not only in the text but in the human condition itself. Maybe the perplexity of the Hebrew grammar mirrors our situation. Here are two very different renderings of verse 10, for example: "I have seen the burden God has laid on the human race" in the NIV. You can feel the weight. To be human is to be weary and heavy laden, beasts burdened from the beginning. To be human is to be Sisyphus: Here's your rock. You will make no progress. Then you will die. Welcome to the human condition. Get to work.

But the NRSV renders 3:10 differently: "I have seen the business that God has given to everyone to be busy with." There's air and light in this version of our situation. A task is "given"; work is a gift. An occupation. This verse almost feels like a brightly lit lobby of an office building, people bustling to work.

Which of these is true of our situation? Perhaps both.

In the next verse, the translators seem to trade their verve. The NRSV is quotidian, pedestrian, businesslike, one might almost say naturalized. "He has made everything suitable for its time; moreover he has put a sense of past and future into their minds" (3:11). This is the language of calendars and chronology, or perhaps a matter of temporal decorum. Humans can count the days, keep track of time, and we know you should never wear white after Labor Day. Time is something we are conscious of, something we think about, something we manage.

But the NIV translators can't resist the legacy of a Shakespearean poetry that sings the fullness of being human: "He has made everything beautiful in its time. He has also set eternity in the human heart" (3:11). In this word picture, time is a frame for things to flower. It's not merely a question of everything finding its slot in the calendar, but creation brought to fruition in time, unfurling and unfolding all its possibilities to attain the beauty always latent there. Rather than the mind simply tick-tocking its awareness of past and future, here the human heart is infused with a time above time, a spark of eternity carried in this temporal vessel.

In spite of what God has put in our hearts and minds, there is so much that eludes us: "Yet no one can fathom what God has done from beginning to end" (3:11). Even with eternity in our hearts, we are temporal creatures inhabiting this mortal vale. The past and future are limited at our horizons. We will never see the whole; we will never have God's scope of perspective. Indeed, we often won't see what's intimate and up close—all that God has done across our lifetime, all the secret ways that God's tending remains hidden.

But our finitude—our lack of Godhood—is not something to resent or lament. Our inability to see the whole is not reason to despair. Our being subject to the conditions of temporality is not a prison but a focus. Gifted with boundaries, we are given room to be happy, to find joy, to enjoy time and—perhaps?—even toil. "That each of them may eat and drink, and find satisfaction ["pleasure" even, the NRSV says] in all their toil—this is the gift of God" (3:13). The Teacher's counsel is provocative, even table-turning: lean into your creaturehood; live into your temporality; dig into your toil. There are gifts you might never have imagined: pleasure, happiness, joy. The delights of a long, hot afternoon tackling the weeds in your garden, rubbing the sweat off your brow with a muddy hand, and the sense of a job well done in God's good earth. The joy of a child's graduation after an arduous trek through anxiety and depressions and a thousand other hurdles. The quiet celebration of a thirty-first anniversary that no one will notice but the two of you, even though, by God's grace, you've turned back generations of brokenness you carried with you, and in your marriage God has done something new in the world.

All these joys are attended by loss. To be a creature is to be passing away, amid things passing away. The Teacher knows this and so reminds us: "God will call the past to account" (3:15 NIV); "God seeks out what has gone by" (NRSV); God will chase it all down and restore what the locust has eaten. Just you wait.

1

# CREATURES OF TIME

## *How to Face Our Forgetting*

> Everything past is thrust back from the future and everything future follows upon the past, and everything past and future is created and set in motion by the One who is always present.
>
> —Augustine, *Confessions* 11.11.13

As she does so often, my wife Deanna has placed a small vase of roses on my desk. They are a gentle pink and smell of apricots. This is day two. They are wilting despite water. Their end is near, but their scent is defiant—a last olfactory burst before dying. Their perfume transports me, time blurred in a way only memory can accomplish. I see a wedding dress and a grave. A beginning and an end.

• • •

I was absorbed by the (sadly overlooked) novel *Ash before Oak*, by a British writer named Jeremy Cooper. The novel takes the form of a fictional journal. The diary, we realize, is an act of survival by a middle-aged man fighting the demons of a suicidal depression on a secluded estate in Somerset. He chronicles the seasons, the rhythms of fauna and flora, with Dillardesque attention to the natural world that feels so near. The entry dated "4 May" contains a simple but moving observation:

> Four rabbits munch on the grass in the old orchard, the setting sun angled so low that its rays shine through their ears. The fallen apple tree bears blossom, I'm astonished to see.[1]

The fallen tree promising fruit. Spring's resurrection among the dead. A loss that produces. This is the arc of temporality.

• • •

From the vantage point of my window seat, descending from thirty thousand feet, I can see a wending river carved through a verdant plain. From this height it is a muddy snake, a liquid road, an ancient path. But then I note something that jars a memory from a high school geography class: what looks like an orphaned bend, as if a liquid amoeba hived off a portion of itself, leaving a horseshoe of water alongside. It's an oxbow lake formed by the persistent erosion of the banks where the river turns. Over years and years, the steadfast current of the river chomps at the banks until, eventually, the S curve leaves a C when the river breaks through, forging a new, straighter channel. The old path that was alive with running water is amputated, sequestered, left behind. The oxbow lake is a geological legacy: set alongside the incessant flow of the hungry river, the oxbow is embanked by sedimentary deposits of the passing water. Without a source, it is now at the mercy of evaporation. Its days are numbered, a reminder of what was visible from the river that is now passing by.

• • •

God's creative word, "Let there be . . . ," started the clock. For everything created, to be is to be temporal, and to be temporal is to be indebted to a past and oriented toward a future. It is to move in a world where things come to be and pass away: events, words, attention, activities all have the characteristic of a kind of passing. As Augustine observes in his reflection on time, language is like an audible clock: communication is possible only if words emerge then fade, making way for the next word in the sentence.[2] We ride the cusp of a wave we call the present, driven by the past and headed for the shore of the future.

But what I'm calling "temporality" is more than just the tick-tock of time's passing. Unlike a shoreline or a statue, human beings are not merely subject to time's passage, the ebb and flow of coming to be and passing away, creation and erosion. Time is not just an environmental condition that impinges upon us like weather. Human beings dwell temporally. Time doesn't just wash over us like rain, because our very being is temporally porous. To be temporal is to be the sort of creature who absorbs time and its effects. A rolling stone might carry no moss, but a temporal human being picks up and carries an entire history as they roll through a lifetime. This is a persistent theme, for instance, in Tim O'Brien's landmark novel *The Things They Carried*. While on one level it is a novel about the Vietnam War, the story compels almost universal interest because it tells us something about the human condition. What he says about these soldiers' experiences is portable in a way: "They carried all they could bear, and then some, including a silent awe for the terrible power of the things they carried."[3]

Time is like another oxygen of creaturehood. The border between body and environment is incessantly open. There is a constant exchange of inside and outside. In the same way that air is inhaled and lives within us, enabling us to live, so time is absorbed as history—not in the sense of past events but as the way time lives on. Forgetting is the exhale of a temporal being, but with every breath, something has been kept.

There is a school of thought in philosophy that has been especially attuned to the dynamics of temporality and the way we are shaped by history. It is called "phenomenology" and traces its roots to a German philosopher named Edmund Husserl. Perhaps the most succinct way to describe phenomenology is to say that it is a philosophy of experience—a philosophical project that tries to understand *how* we experience the world.[4]

Husserl spent a lifetime trying to understand this temporal character of selfhood and identity, and I've no doubt absorbed more from him than I realize. Indeed, this illustrates one of Husserl's key insights: to be is to have been, and to have been is to have bumped up against others who rub off on us. They leave marks we might not always see. More than marks: they leave dents and deposits. Or they drill wells that become underground reservoirs from which we drink even if we don't realize it.

Husserl often invoked the metaphor of horizons—the edges of our world we see when we look in the distance. We are surrounded by horizons that function like a frame for our experience. Our horizons are always indexed to some location. If I am down in the valley, or walking the chasm between midtown skyscrapers, my horizon is limited, constrained. If I climb to the top of the bluff, or drive through the western plains, my horizons swell and expand. But even on that plain, my horizons shift with my location: new sights emerge, others disappear in my wake. Yet even what disappears behind me is carried in me in some way. What I *have* encountered, now in the rearview mirror, primes me for what I *will* encounter.

In the same way that my horizons shift with my body, so I move through time with what Husserl describes as a "temporal halo" formed by the horizons of past and future. Consciousness, he says, is both "retentional" and "apprehensive": we retain a past and we anticipate a future, which is precisely why my own consciousness eludes me.[5] I don't always know what I remember and hope. I am not always aware of what I carry and what I anticipate. The measure of my "I" is always broader than this now of which I am conscious. Every human, as a temporal being, is something like an icon whose possibilities are illuminated by the halo of past and future. Every self has a history. Phenomenology—the method of philosophy founded and practiced by Husserl—is an investigation of this buried history, a philosophical archaeology of the concealed, unconscious life that attends us as creatures in time.

This is probably why there is a natural resonance between phenomenology and psychotherapy. It might also explain why my own experience in therapy opened up new vistas of philosophical curiosity. Eventually I came to realize: my therapist was inviting me, in a sense, to turn my phenomenological tools on myself. That map exercise was prompting me to see the temporal halo of my own selfhood. Husserl offers a technical concept that is illuminating here. My "I," he says, is not just given, a thing of nature; I am *generated*: I am put together, "come about," over time. My self (what philosophers like to call an *ego*, "I am" in Latin) has a history, and at the bottom of the "I" is what Husserl calls a "substrate of habitualities."[6] This "substrate" can be understood as a base layer of experiences that become habits for me and make further experience possible. The history of my own experiences becomes a seedbed cultivated by time so that future experiences have possibilities to grow.

These habits of being ("habitualities") are my ways of being in the world that slowly build up over a lifetime, little deposits and accretions that constitute what I carry.[7] These are not hard-wired instincts; they are dispositions that I've acquired and learned from experience. Opening up the world for me, these past experiences make it possible for me to experience. In that sense, it is my history with the world that propels me into the future. My history makes me "me." The nexus of habitualities that is "me" is utterly distinct, even if I've shared a world alongside a million others. Like my fingerprint or my gait or my retinal map, my temporal halo is a distinct signature of my existence.

On the one hand, these habits of being make my life possible; on the other hand, these habits and dispositions and learned ways of being in the world also come with their limits. Some of my habitualities mean I walk through this world with a limp. I carry them like a burden. Wounds shut down possibility. Some of my formative experiences have disposed me to ignore and exclude, willfully indulging the blind spots I've inherited. Racism, for example, is not just an attitude but a bodily schema of habitualities that I absorb over time.[8] But compassion can become the same sort of dispositional habit, a bodily disposition woven into my very being because I have learned what it means to be vulnerable and to be cared for. Over time, someone has both showed me compassion and showed me how to be compassionate, and my history has been an opportunity to practice my way into being compassionate. Or at least that's my hope!

I love it that Husserl, the fusty German phenomenologist, says that my unique "substrate of habitualities" is the "abiding style" of my identity. Our selves are fashioned; we are adorned with histories that incline us to saunter, swagger, or shuffle.

Given our histories, some of us move through the world with a cape; some of us don baggy sweaters we hide behind; some of us still experience the world as if exposed. The question isn't whether we have a style but which style we've (unconsciously) adopted given our histories. We wear time.

And this is true not just for me or you. It's true for every *us*. These same dynamics are communally and collectively true. As Anthony Steinbock puts it, *who* we are is *how* we are.[9] We share horizons; each collective has its own temporal halo.

Our temporality is sticky: we pick up things along the way—things we need, things we cherish, things that weigh us down. We move through time not just ticking along from moment to moment but with a temporal halo of retention and anticipation. So what does it mean to be faithful amid such flux? What does it mean to be steadfast when, as a creature, I am ever unfolding? Spiritual timekeeping is the way we attempt to reckon with our temporality.

• • •

A feature of temporality that we either downplay or resist is the profound *contingency* of our existence.[10] When we say something is "contingent," we simply mean that it *might not have been*, doesn't *have* to be, and could have been otherwise. And that is true of the entirety of the created cosmos, brought into existence by the free act of a bountiful, loving God. All of creation might not have been. That doesn't make creation random or arbitrary, only contingent.

The contingency at the origin of the cosmos courses through it still. History is the zig and zag of choices and events that both open and close possibilities. Each zig sets a course, each zag charts a trajectory, each choice forges new possibilities and leaves some impossibilities in its wake.

Such contingency is lamented by romantics who entertain fantasies of going back. The movement from "what might have been" to "what has been"[11] is not a fall to be lamented but the arc of creaturehood. The conversion of possibility into actuality is not a loss but a focusing. For every path taken, of course, another was not, and our mercurial souls will sometimes wander back to the fork in the road and wonder. But only stasis could have kept the options open, and for temporal beings, stasis is death.

Possibilities that are actualized have a snowball effect: they build a certain momentum; they become a past that primes us for a future, a trajectory that comes from before us. These are the possibilities into which we are "thrown," as Husserl's student Martin Heidegger once put it. Like the protagonists of *Groundhog Day* and *Palm Springs*, we can have the feeling of waking up and asking ourselves, "How did I get here? How did this become my life?" It is this sort of uncanny experience that Heidegger names "thrownness": the way in which even the life I've made for myself, the accumulation of a thousand choices and decisions, still feels like a life I've been thrown into because, in some fundamental sense, the *possibilities* were also decided for me before I ever emerged on the scene. Heidegger describes this as our existential sense of being "delivered over." This "plunge" into what's been handed down—that range of possibilities to which I've been delivered over—is mostly concealed by our everyday dramas of keeping up, getting ahead, and enduring the tranquilizing effects of mass consumption.[12] That's why, as the Talking Heads attest, you can get through a good chunk of your life before the uncanny experience of asking, "How did I get here?" It's as if I've been hurled into this place, this time by . . . who knows what?[13]

*Thrownness* is a way of naming our experience of contingency. On the one hand, we experience the conditions of our situation as given; on the other hand, we understand that they could have been otherwise. Things didn't *have* to be this way, and if history—mine, ours, the world's—had swerved in a different way, we would have inherited a different set of possibilities and a different configuration of burdens.[14] But the only hand we have to play is the hand we've been dealt by the history that has come before us. Because we are heirs of such history, possibilities open up for us. Thrownness is not a negative thing. Because I've been thrown into the life and time in which I find myself, I have a future that calls for me to realize possibilities latent in what has been handed down. But those possibilities are not infinite, and *what is called for* is also a factor in this handed-down history. That's why we need to take the spiritual measure of William Faulkner's insight: "The past is never dead. It's not even past."[15] Our past is not what we've left behind; it's what we carry. It's like we've been handed a massive ring of jangling keys. Some of them unlock possible futures. Some of them have enchained our neighbors. We are thrown into the situation of trying to discern which is which. We are called to live forward, given our history, bearing both its possibilities and its entanglements. Faithfulness is not loyalty to a past but answering a call to *shalom* given (and despite) our past.

• • •

Contingency means that of every history we can say "It didn't have to be this way" *and* "This is the way it is." The question at the intersection is, *Now what?* How to live forward?

One morning, artist and environmental activist Katie Holten looked at the marble in her bathroom sink and, in its waves and lines, glimpsed what almost felt like a script—a signature in this stone that was the imprint of both time and place, a geological history compressed in rock that was trying to communicate.

This revelation birthed a multiyear creative project she calls "Stone Alphabet." Her goal is to visually transcribe the language of the earth, to hear how the stones cry out. She looks anew at all the stone that surrounds us, listening to the "deep time" of the city. In a notebook she captures the scribbles of marble, the Morse code of granite, the footprints of porous stone, and transposes them into jots and tittles that, in black and white, look like hieroglyphs of the earth telling us a story. "The memory of a rock is of a different temporal order from that of the human social one. While walking Manhattan, looking at the stones, I find myself slipping between past, present, and future." What is this marble saying? What do these cobblestones from Maine whisper, layered on a New York side street? What does the Vermont granite remember here on the exterior of the New York Public Library? "The air is seething with messages, trees are dripping with secrets, stones store stories." In her journal, with a shift of focus performed by unfocusing the eyes, Holten tries to transcribe the subtle languages in the swirl of marble, the patterns of grooves in sandstone curbs, the hieroglyphics we never notice in the limestone at Grand Central Station.

> What can the lines in the landscape tell us? Where are we going? What will we leave behind? Rocks bear witness. All the lines, cracks, holes, marks, dots, wrinkles, and fossil traces that appear in stones over and over again, and on different scales, must be trying to tell us something about the life of the city, of the Earth; about the metabolism of the buildings, of the planet. Messages percolate from the past, up through cracks and scars in the metropolis's skin.[16]

Every day we live amid relics of time. Fossils of our past that live in laws, in institutions, in policies and practices, and in a vast repertoire of habits we inherit from generations that precede us. Just like the rocks that surround us, these cultural and institutional "givens" compose an "action environment" that shapes how we live and move and act. We experience their givenness in the simple refrain "This is how it's done." The very givenness of these realities is a false invisibility: because we don't see them, we are unaware of how we're shaped by such inheritances and how they constrain and channel the way we live.

To speak of these as fossils is perhaps inadequate, even misleading. These fossils are more like zombies because they're still active, half-alive, affecting us. Perhaps they're more like time capsules embedded in the structures of our institutions, churches, and homes—or even better: time-release capsules, embedded histories that keep dispensing over time, like a historical IV drip that nourishes (or poisons) us more than we realize. There are, of course, positive aspects of such invisible legacies. Ancestors with courage and tenacity have made it possible for us to *be*. Immigrant parents or grandparents gifted us with a new set of possibilities in a new world. The generations that created art museums, built our universities, and laid the grids for public utilities keep giving to us. Every time I ride the subway in New York City I am astounded by the audacity of public investment over a century ago—a kind of civic collaboration that is almost impossible to imagine today.

The same dynamic of inheritance is true in the life of faith. Every person who carries a Bible in their hands, a collection of books between two covers, is an heir to the discernment of Christian councils in the fourth century. Our battered Bibles are living relics of their work. So, too, the vast majority of Christians worldwide worship with a repertoire of practices bequeathed to us from centuries past, and our spiritual disciplines carry something of the heat and light of earlier saints in the desert. This temporal inheritance, carried in the artifacts and rituals of the church, is the tangible expression of what we call "catholicity."

There can even be unwitting gifts in a past we spurn. We might believe ourselves to have overcome history with our supposed enlightenment and not realize the extent to which we are living on the borrowed capital of a past that has sustained us.[17] When, for example, movements seek to dismantle the institutions and practices of a democratic republic, whether in a spirit of revolutionary fervor or conspiratorial quasirevolution, they are often not aware of how much their own capacity to do so *depends* on the institutions and practices of a democratic republic. In this sense, the legacies still make possible even the attempt to erase them.

But just as often these invisible legacies—these time-release capsules of the past, these zombie fossils of our heritage—are active in our present in ways that are detrimental to human flourishing. The demographics of our neighborhoods still follow the partitions of redlining in the twentieth century that barred Blacks from owning homes. Freeways are still imposing concrete invaders that decimated marginal communities when planners considered those communities expendable in the name of progress for the rest of "us." All our suburbs with four-lane streets but no sidewalks have bequeathed a world for cars and carbon consumption, inhospitable to humans who might want to walk. The number of women around a board room table tells us that patriarchy is alive and well. Our congregations and denominations still reflect histories of immigration, segregation, and suburbanization.

These zombie fossils of history can be tangible, visceral, carried in the stuff that surrounds us and that we consume. We live off, live from, this environment forged by contingent history. As we ingest it, the fruits of such histories become part of us.

No history is pure; no one's history is pure; what nourishes us is also tainted. You might say that, even as we sit down and give thanks for what's on the table, there is always a legacy to lament too. Every "grace" is a confrontation.

The entanglement of gifts and poisons, grace and lament, is powerfully embodied in the Avett Brothers' song "We Americans." Picture it being sung on Memorial Day or the Fourth of July, when the nation pauses to express gratitude for those who "shivered and prayed approaching the beaches of Normandy" in order to defend a country they love, a country founded as a republic of freedom. But the celebration is complicated, and the narrator confesses it:

> I am a son of Uncle Sam
> And I struggle to understand the good and evil
> But I'm doing the best I can
> In a place built on stolen land with stolen people[18]

The song grapples with what to do with such a legacy, but it can only do so because it faces that legacy. It unearths the history we'd rather bury. And the post-chorus reminds us that all of this is right beneath our feet and on the table: there's "blood in the soil with the cotton and tobacco" and "blood on the table with the coffee and the sugar." The stones cry out, the soil mourns, and the fruit of the earth still groans with the long legacy of its production, a tangible reminder that the creature comforts of many were consumed at the expense of fellow image bearers of God. The only path to a future that is just runs through this confrontation, this confession, this reckoning.

Which is why we are not victims of our history as if the past predetermines our future. "We are more than the sum of our parts," the narrator reminds us, "All these broken bones and broken hearts." We can hope for a future that might be otherwise. Hence the song concludes with a prayer:

> God, will you keep us wherever we go?
> Can you forgive us for where we've been?
> We Americans.

To even ask the question, as prayer, is to entertain a different way of inhabiting time. This song, like a hymn of spiritual timekeeping, braids lament and hope, refusing both nostalgia and despair.

• • •

That we are temporal beings does not decide *how* we relate to time. Unearthing the zombie fossils in our present doesn't necessarily mean we know how to read the hieroglyphs. How to transcribe the alphabets written in stone and sugar, in freeway overpasses and city limit signs? Not every encounter with history is properly a reckoning; not every look to the future is hope.

The question isn't just whether we have a history and a future, or even whether we recognize this; the question is how we relate to our past and history.

There is a sort of fascination with the past that is an act of deliberate forgetting: it's called "nostalgia." Religious communities are particularly prone to this. Faith is "handed down," a matter of *traditio*, and hence faithfulness can be confused with preserving the past rather than having gratitude for a legacy meant to propel us forward. The most significant problem with nostalgia is not that it remembers but what it forgets. "So much of the trouble of this world is caused by memories," wrote Apsley Cherry-Garrard, "for we only remember half."[19] The "past" that is pined for is always selected, edited, preserved in amber, and thus decontextualized, even if this past is invoked as marching orders for restoration and recovery.[20] Whenever the past is invoked as a template for the present, the first question we should always ask is, *Whose* past? Whose version of the past? And what does this invoked past ignore, override, and actively forget? Which half is recalled? Whose half is forgotten?

Nostalgia is rarely antiquarian, a mere interest in history qua history. It is more commonly a sentimental pining for "the way it was." Such nostalgia is always a form of arrested development. For example, there are sorts of nostalgia that are not-so-subtle longings for adolescence and thus resent adulthood. Many forms of collective nostalgia demonize the present while luxuriating in a fabled past. (As Tony Soprano once put it, "'Remember when' is the lowest form of conversation.") But in most cases, and in our collective life, nostalgia usually serves a social and political agenda that wants to reprise a configuration of society that secured a way of life that is being romanticized. All too often, that way of life benefited some—who now remember it fondly—at the expense of others who were ground underfoot by the so-called golden age. In the United States, for example, only white people, most likely men, could recall the 1950s with a rosy glow.

Poet A. E. Stallings grew up in the shadow of Stone Mountain, Georgia—a Rushmore-like, mountainous monument to the "Lost Cause" view of the Civil War, lionizing Confederate leaders on a site that is particularly sacred to white supremacy. Like every monument, it is a particular rendition of memory. Stone Mountain raises the question: What do we do when such renditions of the past loom above us, taunting those oppressed by this "half" of memory?

The sculptor of Stone Mountain, self-taught artist Roy Faulkner, could hardly hide the hubris of his pretensions: he wanted to create a "memorial that will stand through eternity."[21] But even mountains crumble. "A monument is a future ruin," Stallings wryly observes.[22]

Stone Mountain can't be toppled like a statue in a park. But Stallings notes one creative proposal from Atlanta architect Ryan Gravel: "We should allow growth to also overtake the sculpture's many clefts and crinkles as they naturally collect organic material and allow moss and lichen to obscure its details. We should blast it with soil to encourage such growth and consider this new camouflage as a deliberate creative act, transforming the sculpture into a memorial to the end of the war—not to the traitors who led it." In other words, Stallings comments, "to let vegetation weather a monument into a ruin, to let a ruin grow back into a mountain."[23] The ruined monument is a better act of remembering than obliteration. Sometimes the most faithful act of remembering requires a destruction of our nostalgias; sometimes the most creative act of remembering is to ruin the illusions we've learned to live with.

There are similarly disordered ways of relating to the future. The mirror image of nostalgia is a rosy, idealist notion of "progress," a tendency to romanticize the so-called arc of history as the inevitability of our own virtue. In this respect, we tend to imagine our future selves as better versions of our present selves, perhaps because we are blinkered about who we are now. On a micro level, behavioral economists have noted that the choices we make for our future selves seem to imagine we will be different than we are today. For example, when office staff were asked to select a dessert for a lunch meeting next week, three-quarters of them chose fruit over chocolate. But when they selected their dessert at the lunch meeting, the majority chose chocolate. The phenomenon is described as "hyperbolic discounting"—a bias in human psychology that leads us to imagine that the future, and ourselves in that future, will be quite different from the past, despite all the evidence to the contrary (which is to say, despite what we've exhibited in our past up to this point).[24] Such romanticism about the future is like nostalgia in negative. It is not hope but hubris.

Another disordered orientation to the future is what we might call "*doomsday*ism" or what Aquinas simply describes as the vice of despair ("the greatest of sins," in St. Thomas's taxonomy).[25] Rather than romanticizing the future, what is to come is demonized. The mode of anticipation here is primarily fear and alarm (which is why doomsdayism about the future often pairs well with nostalgia about the past). The future is posited as a threat; the arc of history is expected to be always and only decline. There are rapture-ready versions of such doomsdayism, as well as secular forms that find expression in climate apocalypse or political collapse. In the despair of doomsdayism, we are victims of a future already decided and foreclosed. While fixated on the future, such anticipation is the antithesis of hope. When God can raise the dead, not even death is the end. Resurrection and forgiveness mean the future is always an open source of surprise.

• • •

Reflecting on the music of composer Thomas Adès, critic Matthew Aucoin offers a generative metaphor: "History is not a dead weight . . . but rather a still-living, ever-mutating compost heap, a fertile ecosystem within which we forage, hunt, build."[26] History is alive in us and in our institutions. Because our history is never past, *discernment* is a core virtue of temporal faithfulness. We are growing in this compost of history that needs to be sifted: there is certainly refuse to leave behind, but also transmogrifications of our past that are now fertile soil for a different future. Some seedlings are emerging that we might transplant.

If, like the sons of Issachar, we are going to "understand the times," we need to recognize that we discerners are also *products* of time. But recognizing our embeddedness in the vicissitudes of history's contingent twists and turns is only half the work; the other half is knowing how to inherit—what to do with what we've been given. This is the work of discernment.

There is a lesson for us here in the work of German philosopher G. W. F. Hegel. Notoriously difficult and opaque, nonetheless Hegel tried to work out something like a Christian understanding of how the Spirit courses through history, without that turning into some predelineated faux drama, a rigged game that makes history a sham.[27] Watching "world historical" events like the French Revolution, Hegel was trying to discern just what was afoot in these developments. The commentator Charles Taylor suggests that Hegel was reworking a doctrine of Providence. "Against the blithely optimistic eighteenth-century notion of Providence as the perfect dovetailing of a well-joined universe into the purposes of God for man, a vision which Hegel never ceased to treat with scorn, Hegel developed a view of history as the unfolding of a purpose from within, through tragic conflict to a higher reconciliation. . . . History moves to heal the wounds it made."[28] This purpose that emerges "from within" could also be described as a purpose that emerges "from below," a purpose we could only start to see after the fact, when the contingencies of history are in our rearview mirror and we can start to see contrails of events and decisions. This is the gist of Hegel's famous but cryptic statement that "the owl of Minerva begins its flight only with the onset of dusk."[29] Minerva is the Roman equivalent of Athena, the Greek goddess of wisdom. Hegel's suggestion is that wisdom begins to dawn at the end of the day—that we need to get *through* something before the clarity of insight arrives. Only endurance yields wisdom, and often it will feel like insight arrives late. Why couldn't we have known this earlier? That is one of the scandals of temporality.

But even then, we're trying to see at dusk, which is always difficult. Reason squints. As Rev. John Ames writes in Marilynne Robinson's *Gilead*, "Sometimes the visionary aspect of any particular day comes to you in the memory of it, or it opens to you over time."[30] Discernment is the hard work of peering around us when everything is cloaked in the coming shadow of night. Hegel says as much when, just before noting the owl's liftoff, he offers a caution on our hunger for instructions on how the world ought to be. Philosophy, he says, "always comes too late to perform this function." Perhaps there is a discernment that needs to come before philosophy arrives on the scene at dusk. "When philosophy paints its grey in grey, a shape of life has grown old, and it cannot be rejuvenated, but only *recognized*, by the grey in grey of philosophy."[31] But sometimes such recognition is an achievement that puts us on the path to a different future.

The fact that insight arrives late doesn't release us from the burden of discernment. Nor should insight be dismissed because it is almost always hindsight. The Spirit—Hegel's *Geist*—calls to us in history. Discernment is first and foremost not a matter of explaining history but looking to forge forms of life in concert with the Spirit's unfolding redemption in time. Charles Taylor tries to capture this when he says that, for Hegel, the movement of the Spirit is "*in train*" and "it is incumbent on men to recognize and live in relation to it." The movement of the Spirit is something to be joined, which requires something of us. "To recognize one's connection with *Geist* is *ipso facto* to change oneself and the way one acts."[32] And for Hegel, *religious* transformation is at the heart of this: a change in reality is intertwined with a change in consciousness. This is why *discernment* in the midst of history is our central burden: listening for the beat, feeling for the tempo so we can keep time with the Spirit.

There is an important difference between imagining history as a blank slate for our accomplishments and imagining it as a symphony we are asked to play a role in. Taylor's concluding comment is dense but worth considering carefully: "There is a difference . . . between a view which sees widespread willed social and political transformation as something to be *done* by those who would achieve regeneration and a view which sees the relevant social and political transformations as needing to be *discerned* and hence accepted and lived in the right spirit."[33] There's a difference between believing we are the ones we've been waiting for and realizing we are called to join the Spirit of God coursing through history.

I don't think it's overstating it to say these two postures are the difference between hubris and grace. The former—the "something to be *done*" school—is a kind of historical Pelagianism that sees us as the primary actors concocting history by our actions; history will be a history of *our* accomplishments. The latter is more like a historical Augustinianism, a graced temporality in which the Spirit is afoot and on the move and we, by grace, are invited to join and thereby both *be* transformed and be part of the unfolding transformation.

• • •

We are at once caught up in history's unfolding and actors who shape the future. This insight we've seen in Hegel is also central to Reinhold Niebuhr's argument in *The Irony of American History*. Written in the midst of the Cold War, in the face of US hegemony and hubris, Niebuhr cautioned against overestimating our capacity to manage history. At the very moment that we see ourselves as a superpower, actors *on* history, we become blind to all the ways we are shaped and constrained *by* history.

Niebuhr's notion of "irony" is specific, almost technical (not of the Alanis Morissette variety). He emphasizes that our situation—the human condition—isn't merely "pathetic." We aren't simply victims of history who deserve pity as passive "patients" of forces beyond our control. We are both creatures *of* time and actors who *shape* history: "The historical character of man," he summarizes, is that humanity is "both agent in, and creature of, history."[34]

Nor is our condition merely tragic, a situation in which we are forced to make unjust decisions because of some code or environment that befalls us. Our situation, rather, is *ironic*: so many evils are of our own making, and yet so many of those evils are generated by our blinkered virtues and the unconscious shadows of our best intentions. "The evil in human history is regarded as the consequence of man's wrong use of his unique capacities. The wrong use is always due to some failure to recognize the limits of his capacities of power, wisdom and virtue. Man is an ironic creature because he forgets that he is not simply a creator but also a creature."[35] This *failure to recognize* will be an important theme for us, bound up with the importance of discernment.

This ironic understanding of human history is, for Niebuhr, an unabashedly Christian take on the human condition, both because the doctrine of original sin yields a fundamental humility about self-mastery and self-understanding and because irony yields to mercy. He who sits in the heavens laughs with derision at our vain plots, the psalmist says (Ps. 2:1–4). The laughter is derisive, Niebuhr comments, "having the sting of judgment upon our vanities in it." Our situation is laughable, but in God's laughter, which is humbling, there is a warmth and empathy that conveys another possibility: forgiveness. "If the laughter is truly ironic," Niebuhr continues, "it must symbolize mercy as well as judgment."[36] To see the irony of our temporal situation is to see that

> the whole drama of human history is under the scrutiny of a divine judge who laughs at human pretensions without being hostile to human aspirations. The laughter at the pretensions is divine judgment. The judgment is transmuted into mercy if it results in abating pretensions and in prompting men to a contrite recognition of the vanity of their imagination.[37]

Which is to say: the irony of our history always means a different future is possible, both because God can turn the tables ("the stone the builders rejected" becomes the chief cornerstone, Ps. 118:22) and also because recognition can yield contrition—which can, in turn, lead to a change of course. It's never too late for us to become who we're called to be.

Recognition of our situation is the first step. The dawning of a new consciousness is the beginning of a new day. For Niebuhr, it is our failure to recognize this irony of the human condition—the way our actions outstrip our intentions—that leads to hubris. Reality is only too happy to refute such pride. That's why Niebuhr emphasizes that recognition is the beginning of wisdom. Every time our pretensions crash up against a recalcitrant reality, we are being invited to the humility of recognition. Being humiliated by reality can, of course, be an occasion for entrenched fury, a fundamental resentment that the world and time will not conform to our pretensions. But there is always the possibility that such humiliation could be a portal to humility, to a recognition of our limits. Recognition can break the spell: "Consciousness of an ironic situation tends to dissolve it."[38]

That statement from Niebuhr could be the motto of this book, which is meant to be consciousness-raising. This is not a book about what to do with your time, or how to manage your time, or how to redeem the time using some sort of spiritual efficiency. This book is an invitation to a new consciousness of how to inhabit time. "Consciousness of an ironic situation tends to dissolve it": that doesn't mean it *solves* our problems, nor does it *absolve* us from our limits. Recognition doesn't lift us above the vicissitudes of history. It only makes us newly attentive to our conditioning, perhaps less confident in the purity of our good intentions and more conscious of our limited purview, our mixed motives, the ways even our best plans can unravel in unintended consequences in a future we can never control.

Recognition should find its end in contrition—a posture increasingly unintelligible to us in a society dominated by "the liturgy of moral self-appreciation."[39] But if we live with "a religious sense of an ultimate judgment upon our individual and collective actions," this "should create an awareness of our own pretensions of wisdom, virtue or power which have helped to fashion the ironic incongruity." With that awareness, "the irony would tend to dissolve into the experience of contrition and to an abatement of the pretensions which caused the irony."[40] This, I might note, is precisely where the Avett Brothers end "We Americans":

> I am a son of God and man
> And I may never understand
> The good and evil
> But I dearly love this land
> Because of and in spite
> Of we the people

The song is an anthem of recognition, naming the irony of American history; but it ends with an act of contrition, seeking forgiveness, with the hope of living into a different future.

Niebuhr ends, finally, with discernment. "This divine source and center must be discerned by faith because it is enveloped in mystery, though being the basis of meaning. So discerned it yields a frame of meaning in which human freedom is real and valid and not merely tragic or illusory. But it is also recognized that man is constantly tempted to overestimate the degree of his freedom and forget that he is also a creature."[41] When we recognize that we are always embedded in a *when*, a pressing question dawns from this recognition: *When are we?* And where is God in this *when*? Where is the Spirit afoot in our now?

Such discernment is fraught. Niebuhr rightly wonders whether we could ever achieve the "detachment" necessary to read our present, to discern the Spirit's tracks through the history in which we are embedded.[42] To see the irony, one must gain some distance. Is that really possible when we are in the swirling eddy of the present? Niebuhr thinks it possible, and his evidence is the example of Abraham Lincoln. "Lincoln's responsibilities precluded the luxury of the simple detachment of an irresponsible observer. Yet his brooding sense of charity was derived from a religious awareness of another dimension of meaning than that of the immediate political conflict."[43] Lincoln's distance on the situation was made possible by the fact that American history was not the only story he inhabited. His "religious awareness"—which, in Lincoln's case, was a distinctly *theological* attunement—gave him a vantage point from which to see the irony and horror of the two sides of a war who "read the same Bible and pray to the same God," as Lincoln put it in his second inaugural address. Lincoln's recognition of the irony also led to contrition; but such recognition and contrition did not preclude discernment and action. To the contrary, recognition and contrition made it possible for Lincoln, both cautious and bold, to chart a course for action rooted in discernment: that slavery was an evil to be abolished and overcome. This conviction, rooted in discernment, with "firmness in the right as God gives us to see the right."

Discernment always entails risk. Though the work of discerning must be communal, there will never be uniform agreement. The work of discernment is never finished because the Spirit is always afoot in history. To become attuned to the Spirit's song is to change your life.

2

# A HISTORY OF THE HUMAN HEART

## *How to Learn from Ghosts*

> Time is the substance I am made of. Time is a river which sweeps me along, but I am the river; it is a tiger which destroys me, but I am the tiger; it is a fire which consumes me, but I am the fire.
>
> —Jorge Luis Borges, "A New Refutation of Time"

Time is more fungible than you might guess. Because we have quantified and externalized it—in the watch on my wrist, the phone in my pocket, the clock tower on city hall—we are used to assuming that time has been standardized. Measurement is mastery. And such mastery of time has been globalized, with systems of universal translation. A day is twenty-four hours whether in Beijing or Boulder. "And there was evening, and there was morning—the first day." And so with all the days that have followed.

But then a writer like Barry Lopez reminds you that this experience of time is not universal. Even a "day" is elastic, in a sense. Morning and evening don't always arrive. He recounts this dawning realization in an Arctic village:

> As I walked through the village, I realized I had never understood this before: in a far northern winter, the sun surfaces slowly in the south and then disappears at nearly the same spot, like a whale rolling over. The idea that the sun "rises in the east and sets in the west" simply does not apply. The thought that a "day" consists of a morning and a forenoon, an afternoon and an evening, is a convention, one so imbedded in us we hardly think about it, a convention of our literature and arts. The pattern is not the same here.[1]

In such an environment, the declarations of the watch on your wrist feel almost meaningless. Objectivity is not always the arbiter of what is most truly true. If the body keeps score, the body also keeps time. What does a body need and want in the endless night of an Arctic winter? What does such a body remember of its hope when the sun dazzled? Surely the sun is welcomed after the long winter dark. But does its summer refusal to retreat ever become an oppression? Can one crave twilight? We dwellers of earth's temperate regions wonder how one can live in the dark. But does a body incessantly illumined long for night? Is there rest in the dark?

As Lopez notes, this malleability of morning and evening changes what it means to grow. "The Arctic receives, strangely, the same amount of sunshine in a year as the tropics, but it comes all at once, and at a low angle of incidence—without critical vigor."[2] "Objectively speaking," you might say, the Arctic and the equator receive the "same amount" of sunshine. The critical difference, of course, is *when* and *how*. Not even the nonstop sunshine of an Arctic summer can make up for the night. The "same amount" of sunlight is not equally distributed, and given that "virtually all of the earth's biological systems are driven by solar radiation," the differences in our days and nights translate into differences of possibility. What counts as growth is pegged to this elasticity of time.

> Trees in the Arctic have an aura of implacable endurance about them. A cross-section of the bole of a Richardson willow no thicker than your finger may reveal 200 annual growth rings beneath the magnifying glass. Much of the tundra, of course, appears to be treeless when, in many places, it is actually covered with trees—a thick matting of short, ancient willows and birches. You realize suddenly that you are wandering on *top* of a forest.[3]

What if the first eighteen years of your life were an Arctic winter? What if all the sunlight in your life comes late, at an oblique angle? What if the sun cyclically disappears from a life for nights that seem like they'll never end? To grow just one membraned layer under such conditions is a feat. To add another ring—to *endure*—is an achievement. Some years are longer than others.

Don't compare your sturdy temperate trees to your neighbor's Arctic forest. You can't imagine how much implacable energy it took to grow those saplings. You might not be able to fathom what they have endured. You don't know how ancient that forest is, how much time it has spent enveloped in darkness.

Even more importantly: don't compare the trees of your tundra existence to someone else's equatorial rain forest. God doesn't. They live in different conditions. The sun shines upon the just and the unjust, but not at the same angle or with the same intensity. The birch saplings that have punched up through the crust of your prior life are miracles of grace. (Remember when you thought nothing could ever grow there?) They've never lived through your winter. They don't know how long your night has been. By the grace of God, you've endured the dark.

• • •

In the atrium of the Grand Rapids Public Museum, suspended high above the never-ending coterie of school children, is the seventy-five-foot skeleton of a fin whale. Swimming like a ghost through the vaulted space, the articulated skeleton fascinates more than it haunts. In a way, the skeleton suggests only a vague relationship to the daunting mammal we imagine, this hulking collection of bones only an intimation of the behemoth from which it came.

The skeleton has an architecture about it that mesmerizes: a fearsome symmetry, an awful beauty, even if this gentle giant of the deep preyed only on plankton. There is a grace even in these bones, the sensed ease of a creature given to flow. The gray-white of its bone feels placid and pure—as if this were *meant* to be a skeleton.

I had never contemplated the messy violence that rendered a skeleton from the whale that enfleshed it until I read my friend Peter Moe's book *Touching This Leviathan.*

Along with a team of students, Moe—long fascinated by whales—had a dream of recovering, drying, and rebuilding a whale skeleton to hang in the science building at Seattle Pacific University. In his book, he recounts confronting his own ignorance and naivete:

> I thought we would just slice into the whale, grab a bone, and pull it out. The whale has taught me—in the most visceral way possible—that bones are attached to everything. They're

> clothed with muscles, tendons, ligaments, and sinews, and all this must be cut from bone and body. And try as I might, I just couldn't muster the same enthusiasm as these biologists. It's all I can do to keep working. Throughout the day vomit comes up my throat and then returns back again. When it does, I pause, sit up, and breathe the sea air. I'm thankful for the wind.[4]

The biologists tease him: "How do you like that, English professor?" one of them calls. "A lot different than your books, huh?" But maybe not, Moe realizes. "I see myself as reading this body," he reflects, "reading it as I would one of my books, the whale itself a library of sorts, an archive even."[5] The whale's body has a story to tell: in its scars and blubber, in its stomach and ovaries: where she's been, what she's endured. The whale keeps speaking.

And here, even in death, the whale keeps giving. We, of course, have been taking from whales for hundreds of years. Many of their names bear the sign of their usefulness to human endeavors.[6] Perhaps we call them sea monsters—Leviathan!—to justify our vanquishing them. In any case, what the whale yields to human need has sustained civilizations from the ancient Arctic to Victorian London. And here again, washed ashore, the whale's carcass yields her bones to human desire.

Not even death ends the whale's giving. Moe recounts this insight from another whale observer:

> In her essay "The Hvalsalen," Kathleen Jamie visits the University of Bergen's Natural History Museum, which houses a miscellany of whale skulls and bones as well as twenty-four complete skeletons dating to the nineteenth century. Suspended from the ceiling by chains and metal bars, the skeletons still drip oil. "Poor whales," Jamie laments, "don't they know when to stop? The same whale oil that greased the machines and lit the streets and parlours, the oil of soap and margarine. All that oil! Here they were, dead for a century, still giving out oil!"[7]

Our past is not past; it oozes into the present. Skeletons in the closet from generations past still drip, drip, drip into our lives. Sometimes this fuels possibility and opportunity, lighting a lamp for us. Sometimes these bones invisibly drip fuel onto the fire of our anxiety and rage. A buried past is not dormant. Ignoring the past is not a way to escape it. Indeed, the buried past probably takes more than it gives.

• • •

Muscle memory is like a history that lives in the body. Like a well-worn path that runs from the pasture to the barn, over time repeated rituals and rhythms wear a groove that is at once psychological and physiological. It might be chopping carrots or applying paint to a canvas or nursing an infant. What begins laboriously gives way to familiarity. Because we have done this over and over again in the past, we can do it again without thinking about it. An ease and mastery settles in. You could do this with your eyes closed.

Having spent my teen years fanatically devoted to riding freestyle BMX bikes, I can sometimes feel handlebars in my grip like a phantom limb. Sometimes, with my eyes closed, forty years removed from my adolescence, I can remember exactly what it feels like for a bike to leave the safety of a ramp and dare to venture toward the sky. I can feel the pressure of the ramp's curvature as I speed toward the coping. I can hear the lllllllldddddd of my tires on the plywood and then the crisp silence as they leave the ramp. I can still recall what felt like the audacity of flying, but also the flow of my body and bike entwined in the air. The twist of hips and hands to pivot in the sky. The thrilling contortion of a "look back" that would pitch the bike above and behind me as I'd twist to see it before uncoiling and returning to earth. I can tell you that there were moments, lying alone on the couch in my forties, where I would close my eyes and my body would rehearse these movements it knew so well, my legs and arms outstretched, riding a phantom bike, scaling a ramp lost to history.

Sometimes a body remembers what it can no longer do. Muscle memory is not always matched by the muscle's capacity. My body's habits outstrip my body's ability. In the words of that *Top Gun* commander, sometimes my ego writes checks my body can't cash.

Several years ago, no doubt in a pique of midlife nostalgia, I bought a used freestyle BMX bike. The feel of the grips in my hands was immediately familiar. The geometry of the bike felt like a home I hadn't visited in decades. My body was bristling with know-how, with the pent-up memory of tricks like "the lawnmower," "the decade," "the tailwhip," and more. So I rolled expectantly down the driveway to hit the street and unleash my prowess. The ensuing revelation—that will surprise no one but me—was viscerally jarring. The body *did* remember; it just couldn't execute. The humiliation was not just that I was no longer master of the bike but that I wasn't even master of my own body. I am the carrier of desires that outstrip this mortal frame.

Given our histories, our bodies plot stories we can't always live out. We carry habitualities that are anachronistic, out of joint with the time in which we find ourselves. Because we swim in time's flow, our bodies bring habits of intention and desire that don't always align with our present—sometimes they are misaligned with our present version of ourselves. These might be trauma responses harbored from a past life that are wildly out of place in our present, and yet they persist, puzzling those around us. But it could also be an inclination to prayer that catches us off guard because we thought we had left the faith long ago. Or we might pick up the phone to call a friend, seeking communion, only to eventually remember that they died eight months ago. Or we relate to our children as we always have—as fierce protectors, moral guides, life directors—even though they're now in their thirties and need something different from us. It's not just that the past is with us, but that it persists in ways that grate against our present.

This is why you can't go home again:[8] because the you that arrives is not the you that left, and the home you left is not the home to which you return. The raucous welcome-home party for the prodigal won't immediately undo the habits formed in a distant country. But pieces of home went with the prodigal into that distant country, and it was that embedded history that served as his wake-up call to who he was, pulling him homeward.

Our bodies are not just clocks; they are time capsules, but time capsules that, like those dripping whale skeletons, keep emitting possibility in us. The way we experience the world—which is a singular amalgam of environment, experiences, gifts, and traumas—bequeaths to us possibilities, dispositions, desires, hopes that reside in us like spiritual muscle memories. What I aspire to is a factor of what I've inherited. What I imagine as a possible future—even what I can hear as a "calling"—is a reflection of what my past has made imaginable. Our now is always bequeathed to us.

• • •

Every one of us is a Möbius strip of past and future. I think German philosopher Martin Heidegger helps us appreciate this dynamic (an intuition that, no doubt, reflects my own history). Heidegger argues that the very *being* of being human is being *possible*.[9] But this is not blank-slate possibility, merely "empty logical possibility." We humans are always already "attuned" to the world in definite ways. "As essentially attuned," Heidegger says, we are already pitched into specific possibilities.[10] The way I've come through the world means my possibilities for the future have already coalesced in specific ways—like those Arctic forests. This doesn't mean the future is set or completely decided in advance. It's more like concrete in its liquid state: it has been poured into a frame, but you can still make an imprint, shape it by your decisions. Given the ways I've been attuned to the world, my being-toward-the-future has already been calibrated in certain ways, both in terms of the dispositions that I bring and the horizons of possibility available to me. Building on a concept we encountered earlier, Heidegger has a marvelous term for this: *thrown possibility*. The difficulty of the phenomenon he's trying to describe partly explains his somewhat convoluted language, but the insight is worth contemplating despite the difficulty. Here's how Heidegger tries to capture this:

> As a potentiality for being that I *am*, I have let some possibilities go by; I constantly adopt the possibilities of my being, grasp them, and go astray. But this means that I am being-possible entrusted to myself, *thrown possibility* through and through. I am the possibility of being free *for* my ownmost potentiality of being. Being-possible is transparent for me in various possible ways and degrees.[11]

We are bundles of potentiality, but the possibilities are not infinite. We are thrown into a time and place, thrown into a story that is our history, and these form the horizons of possibility for us—our temporal halo we described earlier. That is not a limitation as much as a focusing, a gifted specificity. This corner of earth I've been given to till. These neighbors I am called to love. These talents I'm exhorted to fan into flame.

This neighborhood in which to birth a future. "Go with your love to the fields,"[12] for the horizons that circumscribe you are not fencing you out of something but entrusting you to *this* field of possibility. What's thrown your way is what you *can* do.

And you don't know what's to come. ("No one knows what is to happen," the Teacher counsels, "and who can tell anyone what the future holds?" Eccles. 10:14.) Your horizons are not static because you are essentially potentiality-for-Being. The future keeps unfolding, and what was future becomes the past that launches you into new possibilities. This dynamic of *thrown possibility* keeps unfolding across a lifetime. Formation never stops. My horizons are not petrified at twenty or even fifty. What I can't possibly know are the environmental conditions that are going to be *thrown* my way in the future and how those will reconfigure my horizons. There are still new habits in my future that I can't yet anticipate.

Reflecting on my personal history is like looking at archaeological strata; the layers of my identity are possibilities into which I have lived. What I can imagine, can choose, can hope is a factor of what I've inherited. What it means for me to be *trans*formed is a factor of how I have been formed. I am not a blank slate of willpower; neither am I a robot programmed by a past.

This situatedness of the human condition is no surprise to God, who reaches us under these conditions, within our horizons. Ultimately, to entrust oneself to God is to trust that it is God who has thrown us into this. That doesn't nullify the contingency or specificity of our histories; but it does assure us of God's presence *in* our histories. God's grace does not lift us above the vicissitudes of time's flow; rather, the God who appears in the fullness of time catches all that's been thrown our way in an embrace that launches us into a future that could only be ours because only we have lived this life that Christ redeems.

While repentance is a turning, it should not be confused with nostalgic regret for the life thrown our way. On a collective level, we said that nostalgia is often a romanticized version of a past. On an individual level, while our culture does romanticize childhood and adolescence, there is a more insidious version of nostalgia in negative: *shame*.[13] Shame is a nefarious enemy of grace that thrives on the backward glance. Shame keeps craning our necks to look at our past with downcast eyes, as a life to regret. There are highly spiritualized forms of this fixation that parade themselves as holiness. But in fact this is the antithesis to grace. Shame lives off the lie of spiritual self-improvement, which is why my past is viewed as a failure. Grace lives off the truth of God's wonder-working mercy—my past, my story, is taken up into God and God's story. God is writing a new chapter of my life, not starting a new book after throwing out the first draft of my prior existence. Shame denies that our very being is *possibility*, whereas grace, by nature, is *futural*. Grace is the good news of unfathomable possibility.

God's sanctifying presence in my life doesn't erase what's gone before. Indeed, what God has prepared for me *depends on* what has gone before. My personal history isn't something to regret; it is something God can deploy in ways I never could have imagined.

None of this, of course, explains or justifies the traumas we suffer. Grace is not a retroactive magic that makes evil good. Easter Sunday's light doesn't obliterate the long, dark shadows of Holy Saturday. Grace doesn't justify evil; grace *overcomes* it. That "we are more than conquerors" doesn't make the distress a blessing or the sword a plowshare (Rom. 8:35–37). What changes is who is *with* us and what God can do with our suffering. Shame teaches me to look at my past and see something hideous that makes me regret my existence. In grace, God looks at my past and sees the sketch of a work of art that he wants to finish painting and show the world.

In the hands of such an artist, all my weaknesses are openings for strength, the proverbial cracks that let the light in.[14] Even my sins and struggles hold the possibility for compassion and sympathy. Only such a God could make even my vices the soil in which he could grow virtue.[15] Sometimes only a history of pride and arrogance can yield a profound humility that shows the world something about God. Sometimes being left gives rise to the fiercest commitment to stay. Maybe you grew up in a family where everyone broke their promises and yet, by the grace of God, that has turned into a tenacious resolve to keep your vows. Maybe it's your painful experience of exclusion that makes you such a passionate advocate for inclusion.

Shame wants us to regret our thrownness; grace wants us to see it as thrown *possibility*. Nostalgia wants to undo time, walk it all back, as if this were some sort of recovery. Grace wants to unleash our history for a future with God that could only be ours—living into the version of ourselves that the world needs.

Such nostalgia parades itself as recovery. But it is, in fact, a recipe for loss. The hidden price of getting what nostalgia wants is losing what has been given to you. This is the poignant insight of Nicholas Samaras's remarkable poem "Beloved Ghosts of Geography":

> What would you give to walk again
> down Foxton's Station Road, knocking
> at the door of Lionel Looker's council home?
> What would you give to be four years old again,
> and own God in the adjoining meadow?
> What would you give to see the ghosts
> of village children playing in the school courtyard?
> What would you lose to bring back a time and land

in which everything could be believed?
The security of a village held in time.
What would you leave to live
with your silver-haired father
on the high cliffs of Requa?
What would you give
to have heaven be the way you imagine,
made of the familiar and welcoming?
What you will give is your life
to have your life back.[16]

To walk back a life is to lose it; to get what nostalgia craves is loss. To have your life back would be to lose everything that unfolded and that God wants to use.

Shame—what I'm calling "nostalgia in negative"—keeps looking back, too, but in a way that paralyzes, crushes, disheartens. If nostalgia romanticizes the past as bliss, shame can't imagine a future *for* our past.

Grace, we might say, is like a Sankofa bird.[17] An important symbol of the Akan religion in Ghana, the Sankofa is a majestic bird with its head turned back over its shoulder to look back. But the bird is moving forward, attentive to its past. In its mouth it carries an egg or a seed, signifying life that is to come. It is a fundamentally *futural* symbol, flying forward, bearing the seeds of possibility. The look back is not a longing to return but an awareness of where one has come from in order to live into the future well. The symbol is attended by a proverb, *Sankofa w'onkyir*. A literal translation would be, "Go back and fetch it." In the same way, God does not want to undo our pasts; nor does he want us to nostalgically dwell in our pasts; God's grace goes back to fetch our pasts for the sake of the future.

• • •

Everything we have said about our collective temporality in chapter 1 is also true of the individual. The reality of contingency, our condition of thrownness, and the significance of acquired habitualities that prime our being-in-the-world. The temptations of nostalgia and despair are as real for individuals as for collectives, threatening to distort our self-understanding and how we imagine life in Christ.

On the micro level of the individual, the spiritual confusion of nowhen Christianity manifests as what we might call "blank-slate-ism." Certain myths of conversion feed into this, as if conversion were like the reset of a character in a video game, erasing what has gone before. These forms of ahistorical, atemporal, nowhen Christianity—often hybrid legacies of revivalism and modernism—imagine the "Christian life" as such an utter displacement of the life that I have lived that we are puzzled by the perdurance of habit (which is why it too often morphs into judgmental legalism). Sadly, this often amounts to a spiritualized version of "get over it."[18] The particularities and contingencies of our personal histories are effaced by a version of grace that, rather than saving us, simply obliterates this "I" that has a past.

Of course, "if anyone is in Christ, there is a new creation" (2 Cor. 5:17). Baptism is a burial, and we rise to newness of life (Rom. 6:4). But the new creation is a resurrection, not a reset; we know because of the scars. Just as the resurrected Christ bears the mark of his wounds—his "history" with the Roman Empire—so the new self in Christ is the resurrection of a self with a past. The "I" is saved only if *this* me with *this* bodily history rises to new life. If all that I've lived through was simply erased by grace, then "I" am lost rather than redeemed. If all that I've become and learned and acquired and experienced was just overwhelmed and made null by grace, then salvation would be an obliteration rather than redemption.[19] The God who saves is the God who calls and commissions us to a ministry of reconciliation; and in that call and commission, God wants to unleash the unique constellations of talents and experiences that make me who I've become. When the distinct amalgam of my history—including its traumas and wounds—intersects with the renewing power of the Spirit, a chemical reaction of possibility awaits. That possibility is a *calling*: the "good works, which God prepared beforehand to be our way of life" (Eph. 2:10). Each of us is a singular *poiēma*, Paul tells us: a unique, original, one-off work of art precisely because only this "I" with this history could be the self God can use in this way. Because of my past, God's renewing Spirit can birth in me insights, empathy, attention that are exactly what someone needs in the world.

Grace is not a time machine. Grace is not a reset button. Grace is something even more unbelievable: it is restoration. It is reconciliation of, and despite, our histories of animosity. Grace isn't an undoing; it is overcoming.

• • •

The strange amalgam of thrownness and accumulation that is our temporality plays out in the collective experience of an "us." Who we are is ineluctably bound up with when we are. But it is also true in the microcosm, in the tiny drama that is my life. Owning up to my temporality means facing the legacies of events, environments, conditions, and decisions that got me to this *now*. While each waking moment is alive with possibility, those possibilities are *focal*, given like the horizons in which I find myself: wide, but with limits too. The appreciation of this reality itself takes time. When life is full of possibility in your twenties—indeed, when your life seems overwhelmingly future—it is almost impossible to understand this constraint of a life by its past. Only with a history of decisions does one come to realize what one has done.

This dawning realization is well captured in a scene from Christine Smallwood's gem of a novel, *The Life of the Mind*. The protagonist, Dorothy, is approaching middle age, learning to let go, realizing that possibilities are narrowing, or at least bending in defined directions. Out at the theater one night with a younger friend, Dorothy now sees two very different postures toward possibility, two different ways of inhabiting time:

> Dorothy was at the age where choices revealed themselves as errors, increasingly acquiring the patina of irrevocability. For Rachel, life's tragedies still had a premature, anticipated quality; they were romantic. She looked to the future, careening toward a glorious climax of love or death. Rachel didn't understand the small, bureaucratic, quotidian, present tense.[20]

That "present tense" is still contingent, which means that it carries possibilities. The future is still open. But notice that it is "small," or at least smaller than what it was because of a legacy of Dorothy's own decisions, which were made in situations thrown her way.

Melancholy is a natural temptation upon realizing this, and there is perhaps a distinct melancholy that besets us in middle age when, ironically, something about the past dawns on us. Karl Knausgaard captures the sad ambivalence about this realization:

> Every single moment of life stands open in several directions, . . . as if it had three or seven doors, as in a fairy tale, into rooms that all contain different futures. These hypothetical offshoots of time cease to exist whenever we make a choice, and have never existed in themselves, a little like the unknown faces we see in dreams. While the past is lost for ever, everything that

> didn't happen in it is doubly lost. This creates a particular kind of feeling of loss, the melancholy of an unrealized past. The feeling sounds over-wrought and unnecessary, something to fill our idle and sheltered souls, but it is founded on a fundamentally human insight and longing: everything could have been different.[21]

To recognize contingency without melancholy or malaise is one of the hardest disciplines of spiritual timekeeping.

• • •

Grace, we have said, is overcoming. Not undoing. Not effacing. Not regretful, but overcoming. There is something scandalous about the way God takes up this contingency in our lives—all of it, even the heartbreak and sorrow, the evil and injustice—and forges it into this singular life that is *mine*, that is *me*.[22] It is this *me*, the fruit of zigs and zags, stitches and scars, who is then renewed, empowered, *called*. I am the only one I could be.

None of this justifies or excuses the heartbreak. To be human is to be the product of a history that should have been otherwise: that's what it means to live in a world off-kilter due to sin and evil. And yet now I am the *me* with that history, and without it, I would be someone else.

I can't tell you how many times I have listened to Brandi Carlile's song "Every Time I Hear That Song." Or all the times I've wept in the car or the kitchen. I am not being hyperbolic when I say the song has been like a sacrament to me: it has made me a communicant of a grace I couldn't have known otherwise—an anthem that made the unthinkable imaginable. It is, ultimately, a song of overcoming. But there's a chord of anguish that runs through it. Like a sonic version of Marcel Proust's madeleine, the chord of anguish is released from the tomb of memory by a song.

> By the way, I forgive you
> After all, maybe I should thank you
> For giving me what I've found
> 'Cause without you around
> I've been doing just fine
> Except for any time I hear that song[23]

I can tell you that the first time I heard the song I was scandalized, even angry, that one would offer forgiveness to someone who had caused so much pain. But that anger slowly slid toward astonishment: what a feat of overcoming to have the graced strength to offer forgiveness as an aside! "By the way, I forgive you" as a blessing and benediction offered by one anchored and alive and *strong*.

But then on spin three hundred or so, it was the next lines that began to haunt me: that maybe I should thank the one who did this? (That "maybe" is important: it gets at the dark mystery of what's going on here.) Even this past has given me something, *made* me someone. I am who I am *because of* you and, strangely enough, I've come to love this *me* I've become. Even though you took something from me, in the remarkable economy of God's grace I was given something. So, thank you? Framing gratitude as a question is a way of trying to talk myself into it. To want to overcome is the beginning of overcoming.

• • •

Deeper histories live in us. Every heart is a crypt and a hope chest handed down. We harbor skeletons long buried and aspirations of our ancestors who hoped we'd live out their dreams.

The relics of my grandfather's life might be stored in a box in my basement; but how much of him is carried in me?

Margaret Renkl's stunning memoir, *Late Migrations*, is subtitled *A Natural History of Love and Loss*. The cycles of nature are arrayed alongside the natural history of a family: birth and death, generation and decay, coming-to-be and passing away, joy and grief. Late in the book, Renkl notes something remarkable about butterfly migration: "Monarchs migrate as birds do, but it takes the monarch four generations, sometimes five, to complete the cycle each year: no single butterfly lives to make the full round-trip from Mexico to their northern breeding grounds and back. Entomologists don't yet understand what makes successive generations follow the same route their ancestors took."[24]

Here, we might say, echoing Niebuhr, is the irony of *personal* history: everything I'm able to dream and hope and chase in the future is because of what has been bequeathed to me by those who have preceded me. There is a mystery of inheritance at work here: I am no doubt an heir to dispositions and habits and even pretensions from ancestors I've never met. God's grace enables me to make friends even with my ghosts.

## MEDITATION 2

# ECCLESIASTES 7:10–14

> [10] Do not say, "Why were the former days better than these?"
> For it is not from wisdom that you ask this.
> [11] Wisdom is as good as an inheritance,
> an advantage to those who see the sun.
> [12] For the protection of wisdom is like the protection of money,
> and the advantage of knowledge is that wisdom gives life
> to the one who possesses it.
> [13] Consider the work of God;
> who can make straight what he has made crooked?

> [14] In the day of prosperity be joyful, and in the day of adversity consider; God has made the one as well as the other, so that mortals may not find out anything that will come after them.

How much time passed before the siren song of nostalgia was first sung? Was exile from the garden enough for nostalgia to rear its head? Is it even older? Did Adam ever wistfully recall the peace and quiet of creation, before his mornings were ruined by roosters and the incessant chatter of squirrels drove him crazy, wishing he could turn back time? Did Eve ever brood over pre-serpent times as "the good old days"? Did they commiserate with choruses of "if only" and "remember when" and "back in the day"?

The Teacher is only all too familiar with nostalgia's allure. By the time he pens Ecclesiastes, "Better Back in Egypt" is a classic of Israel's songbook, reprised in new renditions, generation after generation. The Teacher's counsel here is subtle but radical. Don't ask the question "Why were the former days better than these?" he enjoins. The problem isn't the answer, however; it is the question itself. This is a "loaded question" in the technical sense of the term—a fallacious framing because it smuggles in an assumption in the very form of the question itself. To answer it is to buy into that assumption, and it's precisely the assumption that is to be resisted. It's not wise to ask such a question because the question is predicated on a foolish assumption. The Teacher is not chastising curiosity or inquiry; he's not sternly scolding "Don't ask questions!" The Teacher is chastising nostalgia, the foolish assumption that the past was better. That's a foolish place to start, he cautions.

Wisdom, he reminds us, is like an inheritance: it is accumulated, and it is passed on. Wisdom is the unhurried fruit of time served as a mortal. As such, wisdom is, pretty much by definition, what you lacked in "the former days." Every nostalgic impulse to turn back the clock is a foolish willingness to sacrifice all we've learned. Here is the paradox of temporality: to be is to become; to become is to lose and to gain. The "good old days" are only tempting when you forget how foolish you were. You can't go back and keep the advantages you've gained.

You can see how the Teacher braids wisdom and humility here. In a fashion you'll also find in Socrates, wisdom is knowing what you don't know, recognizing what you can't see, relinquishing the hubristic desire to inhabit some space above time. Here is counsel for mortals, for "those who see the sun": Look at what God has done. There is an inexplicable mystery about it. You couldn't have imagined your life, its bends and pivots, its zigs and zags. The crookedness of your unlikely life is not a failure. The wending paths aren't mistakes. The looping route that looked like it was going nowhere was a switchback climbing a mountain. The jagged line that is your story tracks the path of God's companionship and care. Who, indeed, can straighten what God has made crooked? And why would you wish it were straighter? Look what God has done: that crooked line is one he drew with you.

Don't imagine that your times are a measure of God's presence or absence, God's blessing or curse. "When times are good, be happy" (Eccles. 7:14 NIV). And when the times are bad? Again, the counsel to contemplate: "consider." Look. "God has made the one as well as the other." The question isn't whether we're living in some special, divine time. As Annie Dillard reminds us, "The absolute is available to everyone in every age."[1] Time is so democratically experienced not even the plutocrats and billionaires can escape it. The Teacher later describes this with an almost Shakespearean cadence:

> Again I saw that under the sun the race is not to the swift, nor the battle to the strong, nor bread to the wise, nor riches to the intelligent, nor favor to the skillful; but time and chance happen to them all. For no one can anticipate the time of disaster. Like fish taken in a cruel net, and like birds caught in a snare, so mortals are snared at a time of calamity, when it suddenly falls upon them. (Eccles. 9:11–12)

Wisdom is recognizing our mortality, our shared vulnerability, our solidarity in this sea of *chronos*. For we mortals "who see the sun," time is no respecter of persons. But neither is God who, in every time, is as near as our heart (Deut. 30:14).

3

# THE SACRED FOLDS OF *KAIROS*

## *How (Not) to Be Contemporary*

> It is perfectly true, as philosophers say, that life must be understood backwards. But they forget the other proposition, that it must be lived forwards.
>
> —Søren Kierkegaard

In the treasure trove of the church's art, you'll find a number of curious images in which people and places separated by centuries nonetheless appear side by side.

In *The Burial of the Count of Orgaz*, El Greco's monumental painting in the church of Santo Tomé in Toledo, the painter refuses the distinction between past and present as much as he refuses the distinction between heaven and earth. The fourteenth-century mayor of a Spanish town is laid in the tomb by St. Augustine (fifth century) and St. Stephen, a first-century martyr. Despite arriving on this scene over a thousand years later, St. Stephen is shockingly young, and his shimmering golden vestments include a jarring reminder of his stoning. St. Augustine, on the other hand, who is in a way "younger" than Stephen, inhabiting the world centuries later, is here aged but vital, strong enough to hold the armored count as he is laid to rest. They are surrounded by the nobility of Toledo attending the funeral, whose gazes dance on the border between heaven and earth, future and present. Some look downward, contemplating loss; a few glance furtively above, quizzical. It's hard to read their eyes: Are they wondering? Worrying? Longing? Hoping? Can they see the populated heaven above, with Mary and John the Baptist interceding before the ascended Christ, Peter and Paul attending, countless saints alongside floating on lilac clouds?

There's something strange about time in this painting that towers over a space intended for prayer. What El Greco achieves is not simply a bland "eternalization" that denudes humans of their history. Each figure bears the marks of their historical vocation. We know who they are because they wear badges of what they experienced *in* history: Stephen's stoning; John the Baptist's sackcloth; Peter's promised keys of the kingdom. What enables El Greco to collect them all into this one sprawling scene is not a diminishment of history but some kind of curvature in time, bending toward the One who was born to history "in the fullness of time" and who is, at the same time, before all things and the end of all things. When we recall that such images were almost always painted for sacred spaces, Olivier Clément's observation is apt: "The dance of the liturgy does not seek the dissolution of time into a static eternity that is at once pre-existent and co-existent. Instead, the liturgy of the Church unveils and celebrates the true eternity that, rather than being opposed to time, is revealed in the very heart of temporal existence."[1]

In the temporal riot of El Greco's masterpiece, the future touches the present just as resurrection reaches into the tomb. The heaven "above" is also a future *to come*, a future that is now. As one critic observes, at the center of the painting we see an angel bearing Orgaz's childlike soul "through a sort of birth canal of clouds to heaven," in death reborn.[2] The light of that future illumines all the faces looking toward it in the present below. Time here is bent and folded.

One sees similar time-bending in the paintings of seventeenth-century Flemish painter Gaspar de Crayer. In the Norbertine Abbey in Averbode, Belgium, for example, you'll find his 1655 painting *Birth of Christ with Augustine and Norbert*. Alongside the magi, who have laid down their crowns and offered up their gifts, these saints from centuries later kneel before Mary and child. Like a little drummer boy, St. Augustine offers simply his heart aflame. St. Norbert, who gratefully received the Rule of St. Augustine as his own rule for life, offers his veneration. The crèche is collapsing centuries.

In an earlier painting, now in the Vienna Art Museum, de Crayer executes a similar scene that crams centuries into one framed moment.[3] In what strikes me as a special grace, Mary is finally surrounded by women. Mary Magdalen, St. Cecilia, St. Dorothy, and St. Catherine attend her as wise women, bearing gifts of flowers and fruits, the fragrance of adoration that also smells like friendship. Augustine is pictured at some distance to the right, awkward and uncomfortable, as if he doesn't have access to the solidarity these women share. Mary seems a little less interested in his fiery heart than in the communion of these women.

Examples like these could be multiplied almost ad infinitum. Stop in any tiny Tuscan church or Baroque chapel and you are likely to encounter scenes that refuse the rules of history and even the laws of (at least Newtonian) physics. So what is going on in these strange paintings where saints and sinners separated by centuries inhabit the same scene? Is this a feature of ignorance, a quaint relic of a primitive humanity for whom historical consciousness had not yet dawned? Could these painters not tell time? Or is it, rather, a signal of the peculiar nature of sacred time? In these paintings, all created for liturgical contexts, Christian spirituality is the original quantum theory. The burghers of a fourteenth-century Spanish town and the bishop of a fifth-century African city are part of the same worship service. Mendicant friars from the early Renaissance encounter the resurrected Jesus alongside desert fathers. In a chapel, at prayer, the cosmos folds in such a way that Christ and Cecilia are contemporaries.

• • •

This marvelously strange, time-bending imagination of historic Christian faith is radically different from so many Jesus-ified versions of escapism that resent time and romanticize eternity. Too many forms of Christianity merely endure the present as the price to be paid for reaching an atemporal eternity. As Olivier Clément observes, in the scriptural imagination almost the exact opposite is true: "Eternity is oriented toward time." It is most acutely in the liturgy of the church that "time is revealed not as an opposition to eternity but as the vessel chosen by God to receive and communicate the truth of eternity." All gathered together in one frame, these saints across the ages, face to face with Christ and Madonna, bear witness to the sacredness of time as such. "Man cannot open himself to the eternity of God by turning his back on temporal existence. The encounter with the eternal ripens in time, through the lived moments of hope, faith, and love."[4]

The incarnation is the nexus of history and eternity. The collision of time and eternity in Christ has ripple effects for how we understand both, which is why the peculiar Christian imagination is best pictured in painting. The revelation of God "born of a woman" in "the fullness of time" (Gal. 4:4) makes history the arena for encountering God. Time, a creature, is itself primed to be home to its Creator. The divine is not allergic to history. History is already open to the eternal. Time is porous. What is pictured in these paintings is the strange sense that such porosity is horizontal as much as it is vertical: it's not only that time is opened up to the transcendent but also that such incarnational time opens us up to a communion across the ages.

These paintings subtly address a question about the significance of history for living faith in the present. If God's incarnation in history is at the heart of Christian faith, do those of us removed from the event by millennia find ourselves at a distance from God? If the history matters, doesn't that mean the long intervening history creates a distance between us and the intensity of God's presence in history? Are followers of Jesus after the first century always too late to be contemporaries of Jesus?

These questions of time, proximity, and distance are at the heart of Kierkegaard's inquiry in *Philosophical Fragments*, which is ultimately a profound meditation on *contemporaneity* in light of Christ's curvature of time. In the paradox of the incarnation we witness "the eternalizing of the historical and the historicizing of the eternal."[5] The key question that occupies Kierkegaard is just what it means to *see* this paradox: What are the conditions for being a "witness" to this intersection of eternity and history? What if we are not among the happy few who rubbed shoulders with the incarnate God in the first century? Isn't every latecomer further and further away from God's revelation? Does God disappear in the distance like those objects in our rearview mirror which are not as close as they appear? If the irruption of God in history is the nexus of revelation, aren't the rest of us too late to get a glimpse, relegated to a secondhand relationship to God?

The trick, says Kierkegaard, is to neither underestimate nor overestimate the historical. On the one hand, the incarnation of God in history is everything. The incarnation is the fulcrum of the cosmos. Creation finds its fullness in the incarnate God. The enfleshment of God in "the fullness of time" (Gal. 4:4) is the turning point of possibility for being human. On the other hand, the incarnation is not merely a historical event, nor is our proper interest in the incarnation antiquarian or documentary. History matters as a portal to the paradox of the God-man who is then a mirror for facing the mystery of being human.

If we look at these paintings through the lens of Kierkegaard's *Philosophical Fragments*, he offers some helpful distinctions that illuminate something essential to the Christian life. As Kierkegaard puts it, the God who arrives in history as Mary's son in first-century Palestine is not looking merely for eyewitnesses; God is looking for *followers*, learners, disciples.[6] We shouldn't confuse eyewitness contemporaries of Jesus with *followers*. While the historical revelation of God is a condition for encountering the paradox, being contemporary with the God-man is not sufficient for such an encounter. "Knowing a historical fact—indeed, knowing all the historical facts with the trustworthiness of an eyewitness—by no means makes the eyewitness a follower."[7] Why? Because the difference between an eyewitness contemporary and a follower is *how* they relate to this historical appearance. For the eyewitness contemporary, armed with all the historical details, the historical is *merely* historical. It is not a confrontation with the eternal. It is not a *moment* where the appearance of God occasions a confrontation with oneself. No amount of historical detail suffices to make the eyewitness contemporary a follower. Kierkegaard's playfulness here underscores the point:

> If there was a contemporary who had even limited his sleep to the shortest possible time so that he could accompany that teacher, whom he accompanied more inseparably than the little fish that accompany the shark, if he had in his service a hundred secret agents who spied upon that teacher everywhere and with whom he conferred every night, so that he had a dossier on that teacher down to the slightest particular, knew what he had said, where he had been every hour of the day, because his zeal made him regard even the slightest particular as important—would such a contemporary be a follower? Not at all.[8]

In contrast, Kierkegaard muses, imagine some first-century contemporary who was out of town on study abroad, gets back to Jerusalem for Passover, and arrives on the scene "only at the very end when [the teacher] was about to breathe his last, would this historical ignorance be an obstacle to his being able to be a follower if the moment was for him the decision of eternity?" Not at all. "For the first contemporary, that life would have been merely a historical event; for the second one, that teacher would have been the occasion for understanding himself."[9] History matters, but *how* it matters makes all the difference. Historical proximity is not the same as an encounter with the God who arrives in history. Being alongside the teacher does not suffice. Rubbing elbows with the incarnate God on the subway doesn't make one a disciple. The incarnation is oblique: if the contemporary "believes his eyes, he is in fact deceived, for the god cannot be known directly." But if this is the case, "then what is the advantage of being a contemporary?"[10] None, in fact.

This is where Kierkegaard introduces one more illuminating distinction. When this God arrives in history, the call isn't merely for believers but *followers*. "Come, follow me" is the invitation. The question isn't just a matter of what they see or believe but what they do in response. Kierkegaard distinguishes contemporary followers—those first-century eyewitness disciples who lived in historical proximity to the Messiah *and* recognized him as the incarnate God—from "followers at second hand," those latecomers whose encounter with the incarnate God depends on the eyewitness testimony of those contemporary followers.

It's natural, says Kierkegaard, to imagine that the first generation surrounding Jesus enjoyed an advantage, a privileged access to transcendence—the fortunate ones "timely born," as it were, who received the bread and wine from Jesus's own hand. But the manifestation of God is not available in the way a billboard announcement is. The Creator of the cosmos comes at us slant. He shows up in a way that also hides. God's self-communication, as Kierkegaard would put it, is always indirect, which means it takes more than ears and eyes to see and hear. God can come to the creation he made and yet not be received or perceived (John 1:10–11). When God empties himself, humbles himself, taking the form of a servant, the revelation is oblique (Phil. 2:6–7). On the road to Emmaus, not even resurrection immediately translates into recognition; something else has to be given. There is a grace needed to glimpse the God who graces history.

God's self-revelation in history means everything, but that only becomes an encounter with the paradox of God-come-near if God grants the condition to see the Son in the servant. So "let no innkeeper or philosophy professor fancy that he is such a clever fellow that he can detect something if the god himself does not give the condition."[11] The encounter with the eternal could only happen in history, but God's revelation could never be extrapolated from history, deduced from the facts by some religious Sherlock Holmes.

Thus, Kierkegaard points out, "one can be contemporary without, however, being contemporary"; one can be "contemporary" in the usual sense of historical proximity and, in fact, be a "noncontemporary" of the God who appears.

> What else does this mean except that one simply cannot be immediately contemporary with a teacher and event of that sort, so that the real contemporary is not that by virtue of immediate contemporaneity but by virtue of something else.[12]

That is why "someone who comes later must be able to be the genuine contemporary." In other words, there are ultimately no "followers at second hand," because anyone who is going to encounter the paradox, whether in AD 33 or 1843 or 2023, needs the perceptual grace, granted by the same God, to see around corners, to catch what's told slant. The epiphany of the paradox cannot be achieved by bottom-up speculation, even from the historical facts. The indirect communication that is the incarnation requires something we lack, an illumination only God can provide. And insofar as only God can provide that to each of us, each follower is in direct relation to the Absolute. Someone "who comes later must receive the condition from the god himself and cannot receive it at second hand." And "if the one who comes later receives the condition from the god himself, then he is a contemporary, a genuine contemporary."[13]

You could say there are no latecomers in the communion of the saints, which is just to say that *all* of us are latecomers to the arrival of a hidden God. This eternalizing of the historical and historicizing of the eternal at once sacralizes time and flattens *chronos* because it is "the moment"—*kairos*—that makes all the difference. Thus Kierkegaard sees the God who grants the condition as the reconciler of all generations.[14] God is no respecter of ages. To repeat Annie Dillard's phrase, "the absolute is available to everyone in every age" insofar as both the contemporary follower in AD 33 and the follower-at-second-hand in 1843 are in immediate relationship with the Absolute. God is as near to the twenty-first-century disciple as to the medieval saint. And the medieval peasant is as near to God as the first-century apostle.

Now those paintings we started with make sense: the hub of every image is the immediacy of Christ to every generation. In the paradoxical calendar of incarnational time, the distance of *chronos* is drawn near by the intimacy of *kairos*. This is not an evisceration of history as much as a curious kind of compression: not history *or* eternity, but eternity *in* history and hence a gathering up of history by the eternal God who stoops to inhabit time.

• • •

In Christine Smallwood's novel *The Life of the Mind*, Dorothy is consigned to academic limbo, toiling as an adjunct lecturer, wondering, like Dante, if she'll be able to climb out of this purgatory to the *paradiso* of the tenure track. When we meet her, she has just suffered a miscarriage, which Smallwood evokes with writing that is tactile, viscous, and unabashedly bodily.

The novel is a profound meditation on endings; or how we know when something has come to an end; or, perhaps better, whether we're willing to face what we know is the end. How to let go. How to say goodbye to an ambition. How to live with loss. "She lived in an epilogue of wants," the narrator says of Dorothy. Which, perhaps, is just to say that this is a novel of middle age ("Dorothy was at the age where choices revealed themselves as errors, increasingly acquiring the patina of irrevocability"). But it's hard to resist a broader, almost allegorical reading about the American experiment: Would we recognize the end if we were living it?[15]

There is a somewhat surprising, matter-of-fact presence of religion in Smallwood's novel. Dorothy is teaching a course called "Writing Apocalypse," which is an occasion to revisit Jonathan Edwards and the book of Revelation to try to discern the difference between the "texture of *kairos*" and the "gruesome slog of *chronos*."[16] In fact, this question of the understanding of time governs the novel's narrative. Dorothy is always noting different kinds of time (like "pet time" or "airplane time"). She's waiting for the unveiling. It turns out you have to endure a lot of *chronos* before you know it's *kairos* o'clock—that the end has arrived. On the other hand, just as Dillard suggested, any moment is susceptible to irruption: *kairos* attends *chronos* as an ever-present possibility.

"It's hard to know when something ends," Dorothy says late in the novel.[17] But maybe this isn't just because of our own myopic inability to recognize the end; maybe it's because, with *kairos* hovering over everything, you never know when an ending isn't the end. When the dead are raised, not even death is the end. The question isn't "What time is it?" but "*Which* time is it?" The absolute is available to everyone in every age. Any blip of *chronos* holds the possibility of being *kairos*, a moment pregnant with possibility. As Daniel Weidner has said, speaking about the theologian Paul Tillich, *kairos* means "every moment might be the small gate through which the messiah will enter."[18]

• • •

Like the paintings of El Greco and de Crayer, Christian liturgy enacts the sacred folds of *kairos*. The liturgical calendar rehearses the way time curves and bends around the incarnate Christ like a temporal center of gravity. Year after year, during

Advent, the church relives the messianic hope of Israel, awaiting the promise—and it has been doing so for two thousand years since the Messiah was born in Bethlehem. Every year, the church walks with Jesus toward Gethsemane, bears witness to his anguish and suffering, steps again into the chilled shadow of the cross, lives with the harrowing silence of Holy Saturday, and arrives on Easter morning to witness the explosion of light that is the resurrection of the Son of God. For millennia, the church has followed the magi over and over again, seeking the threatened King. Two thousand times and counting, the church has been perplexed by the ascension and then stakes its life on Pentecost.

For those unfamiliar with liturgical time, this will seem to be a recipe for boredom. ("*Again?*") It is perhaps misunderstood as if the point were simply to remind us of what happened, as if the liturgical calendar were merely a memorial device. But it is something more enchanted than that: it is an invitation *into* the event, an experience of Kierkegaardian contemporaneity. When, in a Tenebrae service on a Good Friday, candles are extinguished with each of Christ's last words from the cross and the shadows begin to swallow us, we are not invited to merely remember a "historical event." We are invited to inhabit time in such a way that we are there and then. When the last light is extinguished and the terrifying strepitus roars across the silent dark, we are bereft. A solo voice might then ask the time-bent question of the Black spiritual: "Were you there when they crucified my Lord?" which, in a turn befitting El Greco, pivots to the present tense: "O sometimes it causes me to tremble!" There will be years when the "Hallelujahs!" of an Easter morn are not just reenactments of the past but fresh realizations of a soul that has spent a year in the pit, all too familiar with Sheol, for whom the possibility of living again has been experienced as if for the first time. The resurrection is *now*, and in the now you hear a God who says, "Awake. Breathe. Live. I want you to be."[19]

This annual rehearsal of incarnation and passion is only "repetitive" in the Kierkegaardian sense of a repetition *forward*, a return that generates new possibilities.[20] Perhaps we could say that the Christian inhabits time as cyclical *and* linear. Like light that is both wave and particle, the event of the incarnation makes a decisive dent on the calendar—there is no going back once the Creator God has made himself a creature subject to the vicissitudes of time. The incarnation is a revelation that leaves archaeological traces. There is a before and after of God's arrival in the Son. History has unfolded, even "progressed."[21] But on the other hand, the rhythm of the church's worship—which is the very cadence of the church's life, the heartbeat of the body of Christ—spirals forward by living back into humanity's encounter with the incarnate God in time. In the timekeeping of the people of God, it is Christmas *again*, Easter *again*, Pentecost *again and again*.

This kind of folding of time has always been a characteristic of the people of God. In the introduction to his translation of the book of Deuteronomy, literary scholar Robert Alter highlights the way that Moses's rhetoric speaks to a later generation, who were about to enter the land, as if they were the generation that fled Egypt and crossed the sea—despite the fact these events happened a generation earlier. "The Lord our God made a covenant with *us* at Horeb," Moses tells an assembly who couldn't have been there. "The Lord spoke with you face to face at the mountain, out of the fire" (Deut. 5:2, 4). In the vivid descriptions of the trials of Israel and Yahweh's enduring faithfulness, Moses's speeches make later generations witnesses of past events in the same spirit that Kierkegaard's later followers are "contemporaries" of Christ. "At one remove, the members of the historical audience of the Book of Deuteronomy are implicitly invited to imagine what their forebears actually saw, to see it vicariously. The midrashic notion that all future generations of Israel were already present as witnesses at Sinai is adumbrated, perhaps actually generated, by this rhetorical strategy of the evocation of witnessing in Deuteronomy." Alter describes this as a "slide of identification between one generation and another. Most of those listening to Moses's words could not literally have seen the things of which he speaks, but the people is imagined as a continuous entity, bearing responsibility through historical time as a collective moral agent."[22]

To say that Moses's folding of time is invoked as a rhetorical strategy is not to make it a fiction. The rhetoric reflects a reality about a people—what we might describe as a "social ontology," the co-inherence of the people of God across generations.[23] There is a real and significant continuity of a people constituted by the covenant. This binding of a people across time and generations is the same reality expressed in the communion of the saints. The later generation lives into specific possibilities because of what it has inherited from those who crossed the sea and wandered the wilderness. This continuity is real because of the enduring presence of the same God to whom all generations are connected, and also because habitualities are collective as well. Hopes are inherited; so are idolatries. Just as agency is bequeathed and inherited, so responsibility bleeds across generations. This conception of time—this "sliding" between generations—fundamentally rejects the atomism assumed by individualism, a conception of both self and community that makes each individual a discrete unit. The Bible is riddled with second-person plural pronouns that situate us in a communal reality, and that community is continuous across time.

Hence the relativization of chronology. Wave and particle. The present matters, but *now* is not only the present. Our *now* is pregnant: it bears possibilities from a past that will be borne into a future. The time stamp of a generation's existence is caught up and enfolded into an ongoing reality that both precedes and follows us. The generation of Israel standing on the shore of the Jordan is defined by that part of its "body" that wandered in the wilderness. The past generation's experience is *in* them, a defining part of who they are as they embark on this possibility. And to be who they are called to be in the promised land, they must remember who they are.

Time, for the people of God, is both linear and cyclical. What unfolds in history matters. There is no turning back the clock. Yet we do revisit those events in our now as a matter of orientation, resynchronizing our internal and collective clocks, so to speak—to remember *when* we are. Our relation to those people-defining events is, in some significant sense, more defining than the swirl of current events in which we are immersed. Karl Barth famously invited us to read the Bible with a newspaper in the other hand, but many seem to misunderstand his point: it is the Bible that positions the front page, not vice versa.

In many ways, modernity is the triumph of the line over the cycle. Since the eighteenth century, we've been trained to visualize time's march in the form of a line. In 1765 the English chemist Joseph Priestley published the first of what we would now easily recognize as a "timeline." In an accompanying pamphlet, Priestley conceded the mysterious ethereality of time but argued that, nonetheless, "it admits of a natural and easy representation in our minds by the idea of a measurable space, and particularly that of a LINE."[24] The visual metaphor is not neutral. The image of time as a line is an interpretation. The line is a measure of progress, leaving behind ignorance and naivete to achieve enlightenment and mastery. Onward and upward. The timeline, Daniel Rosenberg observes, "amplified conceptions of historical progress that were becoming popular at the time," despite the fact that history "had never actually taken the form of a timeline or any other line for that matter." The visual simplicity of the image, which made it so effective, was also the problem: the simplicity was an illusion "to support the fantasy of linear time."[25] The line erased all the zigs and zags of contingency, the steps backward, the debts spiraling forward, as if one could map the Amazon with no bends.

Henri Bergson, the great turn-of-the-century phenomenologist of time (Proust was best man at his wedding!), decried this fantasy for the "idol" it is.[26] Linear progression is not how we experience time, either individually or collectively. Our *experience* of time is one of "duration" (*durée*). This is a kind of succession without separation, what Bergson describes as a "melting" (akin to Alter's "slide"). Past and present permeate each other; the *now* is porous.[27]

At the same time that Bergson was making this point, Einstein was demonstrating that time is relative. Modernity always generates its own countermodernities. Together, Bergson and Einstein challenged the simplistic linearity of "modern" time. In doing so, they point us back to something like a Hebraic conception of temporality, where the line between the Moses generation and the Joshua generation is blurred and bent in such a way that those who cross the Jordan are addressed as those who also passed through the sea. "We" are longer than our lifetime.

• • •

Since time is bendable and relative, a constructed way of ordering our lives, it makes a big difference which clock and calendar you live by. There is no objective or absolute time, which is why there can be rival calendars and clocks in tension. Once while my wife and I were staying on Michigan's west coast, on the very edge of the eastern time zone, we started to notice that our phones and smartwatches seemed to flip back and forth between central and eastern time, perhaps weirdly picking up some bouncing cell signal across the lake. Eventually this happened enough that, without old-school watches on our wrists, we were at a loss to know what time it "really" was.

It's easy to forget how much our clocks and calendars are the productions of convention, the legacies of contingent decisions that could have gone otherwise. Which is just to say, we often don't realize how contested time was before 1884, when the International Meridian Conference met in Washington, DC, to forge an agreement on time and calendrical calculation.

Up until that point, time seemed to be "natural," indexed to the sun and stars ("solar time"). But as continents became increasingly interconnected, first by shipping and then by railroads and telegraph across the nineteenth century, the dizzying array of "local" times began to clash. In fact, allowing localities to follow "natural" ("solar") time proved deadly: the spectacular crashes of trains sharing the same tracks were a primary impetus for standardizing time.[28] The demands of transatlantic and transcontinental commerce and industry were another prime motivator.

Efforts at standardization were originally regional, then national. For example, beginning in 1833, the Greenwich observatory on the Thames would raise a "timing ball" at 1:00 p.m. for all ships docked in the harbor to see, an opportunity for visual synchronization. The expansion of railways in the United States eventuated Standard Railway Time with five time "belts" across the continent. (In France, railway companies used a standardized time that lagged five minutes behind Paris solar time as a kindness to unpunctual travelers.) The installation of a transatlantic telegraph cable in 1851, connecting Europe and North America, "was perhaps the single most important achievement in internationalizing the time system."[29]

Which is when the real fights began. *Whose* time would be ground zero, so to speak? More technically, where would the prime meridian—the point from which everyone else would count—be located? France lobbied for Paris; Britain pointed to the groundbreaking science at the Greenwich observatory; others proposed a "neutral" location in the middle of the Pacific, 180 degrees from Greenwich (the French saw what they did there). The US Congress eventually convened the International Meridian Conference in 1884 where, after much haggling, deliberation, and negotiation, forty-one delegates from twenty-five nations agreed to make Greenwich the prime meridian. Subsequent negotiations agreed on a global, twenty-four-zone time system, establishing the longitudes for our current time zones. The delegates, resisting naval convention and affirming civilian sensibilities, also agreed that the so-called universal day would begin at midnight. They even had to come to an agreement on just what constituted east and west on a spherical planet, eventually settling on the 180th meridian as the international date line.

In other words, pretty much everything we take for granted about time is a matter of convention, which is why historian Lewis Mumford could argue that "the clock, not the steam-engine, is the key machine of the modern industrial age."[30]

We're all choosing to synchronize our watches with someone's configuration of time. We're all counting the days based on some calendrical convention. Pick your calendar wisely. The answer to the question "When are we?" is determined by whose "timing ball" we're watching. Even if time has been standardized in the twenty-first century, that doesn't mean there aren't still rival calendars vying to set the standard of our life. The church's worship, organized by the cadence of the liturgical calendar, is a calibration technology for the soul and the larger body of Christ. In Sojourner Truth's memorable phrase, the liturgical calendar reminds us "what time of night it is."

Time's relativity and the now's porosity is lived out liturgically in the church's worship. To be constituted as such a peculiar people requires a strange sort of synchronization of time. Like operatives launching a mission in a spy thriller, coordinating their watches so they're all on the same time, the people of God synchronize their soul clocks in relation to a story that cycles and repeats in the liturgical calendar. In the liturgical calendar, we are indexed to the solar time of the Son who is the light of the city of God (Rev. 21:23).

• • •

Or, instead of the technics of synchronization, think of the give-and-take of a dance and what it means to *follow*. In an illuminating essay, historian and academic Clair Wills invites us into what social dancing—"partner dancing"—feels like. "In partner dancing," she begins, "there is a leader and a follower, and early on I realized that the obvious choice for me was to learn to follow" because, without realizing it, for years she'd been covertly training to follow. How so? Because "following is reading." To follow is to read a partner, and Wills has spent a life reading.[31]

This twosome, it turns out, is fictional. Each dance, she observes, is collaborative, but "there are actually two leaders. One is the person you are dancing with, who leads you through a series of figures in time with music. And the other is the music itself. The task of the follower is to listen to both of them, to hear them, and to respond creatively in turn." Following is not passive or automatic; it is its own creative act, reading the body of another, finding the rhythm of the music, listening for what is called for. "The couple," it turns out, "is a triangle."

Time is carried in the music, and the leader is listening, but the follower is both listening and feeling for the signals in a hand on one's back, a caress on one's side. "When dancers dance socially, a follower's every move is of necessity a split-second late." That is not a failure; the gap cannot be closed. "The dance is in the delay."

Posture becomes the follower's tactile radar. The art is in the response. Wills captures this beautifully and suggestively:

> A follower is all antennae. She, or he, must cultivate a kind of active uncertainty, a positive doubt. She must be relaxed enough to feel the slightest of cues from her partner, and yet sufficiently poised, mentally and physically, to be able to play—to respond, to hold back, to make form out of commitment, interruption, and hesitation. Her weight must be finely balanced so that she can answer the call to step or turn this way or that, as though she had anticipated it, yet without having known what was coming.

The dance is ephemeral. In five minutes the music stops. But now that dance is carried in you. "Another kind of past is held in the body of the dancer herself," says Wills. "What gets called 'muscle memory' is just part of it. The memory into which you step as you begin to dance includes all the dances you've ever danced before, all the partners you've ever had, all the practice you've put in, all the music you've listened to." But the dance is in the moment. "The joy of dancing as a follower is to listen for the barely said."

Imagine the church not like a railway timetable but as a dance hall. Every worship service is practice for dancing into the world. The bride of Christ is invited into the distinct, creative joy of following, attentive to the leader, listening for the music. Poised, attentive, attuned: What now? What next?

# 4

# EMBRACE THE EPHEMERAL

*How to Love What You'll Lose*

> Where are the songs of spring? Ay, Where are they?
> Think not of them, thou hast thy music too
>
> —John Keats, "To Autumn"

We are driving through Pennsylvania's Susquehanna Valley. It is late October. The autumn sun is spread across the hills, its illumination tinged with descent. The crisp air is a reminder: winter is coming. But today this valley is on fire. We are surrounded by trees enflamed in reds and oranges. As we ascend, shades of goldenrod and pumpkin give way to umber and brown, as if the leaves are burnt, spent. In this light, even the stark, scraggly branches are somehow beautiful in their barrenness. We are witnessing the end. All this autumnal beauty is a halo around winter's death and dormancy. This sublime enchantment is a last act, a valedictory display only possible because these leaves are starving. They will not go gentle into the night but blaze against the dying of their light. And here I am: stunned and grateful for their spectacular demise. Their long green life was only a prelude to this fierce pageant.

It is perhaps not accidental that I had this epiphany just days after my fiftieth birthday. My attention was also no doubt primed by a pensive column by the writer Margaret Renkl about the feeling of fall in the late chapters of a life.

> Perhaps the reason I didn't feel sad about the onset of fall when I was younger is only that I was younger, with my whole life still ahead. In those days my only worry was that my real life, the one I would choose for myself and live on my own terms, was taking too long to arrive. Now I understand that every day I'm given is as real as life will ever get. Now I understand that we are guaranteed nothing, that our days are always running out. That they have always, always been running out.[1]

Her autumnal yard is a mirror, and she feels an affinity with all the creatures scurrying against the waning light, sympathetic to "the comical shabbiness of the bluebirds in molt," admiring the hummingbirds battling over the feeder as they fuel themselves for migration, awed by the spider who is greeting her end with one more spectacular web in which she'll leave her legacy: "the perfect egg sacs she has strung together like pearls." She is making way; she is letting go; she is leaving the world these pearls of possibility.

• • •

The French poet Charles Baudelaire suggested that modernity was fascinated with "the ephemeral, the fugitive, the contingent."[2] Rather than painting stolid landscapes, modernist painters attend to the ballerina's leap, the exhale of steam from the train, the golden light before the sun plunges again beneath the horizon. In this sense, modernism could be seen as an intense attunement to creaturehood and the lineaments of the human condition. To be created is to be ephemeral, fugitive, contingent. To be a creature is to be a mortal, subject to the vicissitudes of time: the sun rises and bids farewell each day; the tulip bulb pushes forth, blooms in glory, and then passes into hibernation; we learn, remember, forget. Learning to be a creature is a matter of learning to let go.

The recognition, even embrace, of the ephemeral should be at the heart of a Christian temporal awareness. Imagine embracing the ephemeral as a discipline of not only conceding our mortality as a condition but receiving our mortality as a gift. It is winter's loss that grants us fall's fire.

Our finitude is not a fruit of the Fall (even if it is affected by the Fall).[3] Contingency is not a curse. To live in resentment of creaturely finitude is its own form of pride. Of course, there is much to lament in many of our losses. We are robbed by the brokenness of the Fall. But not everything that fades has been stolen. Not all passing away is an outworking of the curse. Learning to live with, even celebrate, the transitory is a mark of Christian timekeeping, a way of settling into our creaturehood and resting in our mortality.

To resent mortality is a mark of hubris. When we resent our own mortality, we resent the fact that what is given is not eternal. Then, all too often, we try to fabricate eternity: we cling and dig in our claws, refusing to let go. The irony is that we lose in grasping. Sometimes it is precisely when we try to seize and freeze what is passing that we abjure our creaturehood and lose something that is right in front of us.

In 2019, after a long and tormented hiatus, Tiger Woods roared back to his winning ways in professional golf. At the time, a photojournalist pointed out a stark difference between an early win in 1997 and his latest triumphs in 2019. The image of the eighteenth hole in the 1997 photograph has the feel of a Renaissance masterpiece: a portrait of a sea of faces as if illumined by Caravaggio, variously rapt, gasping, roaring, all fixated and focused on the ball as it plummets into the hole, securing the win. The gallery watching was like one organism. No one there will ever forget Tiger pumping his fist in the air, a young conqueror.

This image was then contrasted with the 2019 event. Tiger is still surrounded by a sea of people on that final hole, but their eyes are elsewhere: they are looking at their smartphones as they freeze this moment in a photograph, focused on clicking at just the right instant. The faces are obscured by upstretched arms, and a thousand tiny replications of the event float above their heads. Bent on capturing the moment, they are no longer present to it. Determined to hold on to the experience, they miss the opportunity to experience it. The moment is lost by the desire to seize it.

This contrast reminded me of a remarkable insight in photographer Sally Mann's memoir, *Hold Still*. She is reflecting on the death and loss of two beloved men in her life: her father and a dear friend, artist Cy Twombly. Her memories of Twombly are vivid: she can immediately recall "his drawling voice, his wrinkled face, the gap between the front teeth—Cy is right here." His presence can be invoked by memory itself. But then this surprising observation from a professional photographer: "I am convinced that the reason I can remember him so clearly and in such detail is because I have so few pictures of him." Twombly lives in her, a companion of memory, in a way very different from her father, she admits: "Because of the many pictures I have of my father, he eludes me completely. In my outrageously disloyal memory he does not exist in three dimensions, or with associated smells or timbre of voice. . . . I don't have a memory of the man; I have a memory of a photograph." The father captured on film is lost to her; the friend remembered is present. Mann diagnoses why our ability to freeze-frame reality is actually a loss:

> Before the invention of photography, significant moments in the flow of our lives would be like rocks placed in a stream: impediments that demonstrated but didn't diminish the volume of the flow around which accrued the debris of memory, rich in sight, smell, taste, and sound. No snapshot can do what the attractive mnemonic impediment can: when we outsource that work to the camera, our ability to remember is diminished and what memories we have are impoverished.[4]

I have tried to absorb Mann's insight into my own rhythms and practices. It's mostly a matter of giving myself opportunities to remember rather than turning every experience into something to be archived. The penchant to capture every instant of beauty on my iPhone becomes a way of losing the world. Rather than living with me in my visceral memory, all the joy and beauty I experience ends up buried in a photos folder I rarely look at. The result is a diminished experience of both present and past. When I'm bent on capturing the moment in a snapshot, I am less present to the present; I'm fixated on a future memory—which ends up being a sad substitute for an emotion or vision I can carry in the caverns of my soul.

So I've adopted a simple practice: I intentionally leave my phone behind when I venture into spaces of beauty or when I'm anticipating a momentous event. I want to be present to the present precisely so it will be alive to me as a future memory. Whether I climb to the sublime perch of Circle Bluff overlooking the Frio River in the Texas Hill Country, or am enjoying intimate candlelight with Deanna at a café in Nice, I want to be present to the present, to luxuriate in the *now* without the anxiety of losing it. By giving myself over to the moment, I can carry these joys with me in ways I couldn't have imagined.

To be temporally aware of our creaturehood is to wear mortality comfortably. To live mortally, we might say, is to receive gifts by letting go, finding joy in the fleeting present. This is temporal contentment: to inhabit time with eyes wide open, hands outstretched, not to grasp but to receive, enjoy, and let go. Sometimes knowing this won't last forever compels us to hold hands in the present.[5]

• • •

Christian timekeeping is like a dance on a tightrope: on the one hand, we are called to inhabit time in a way that stretches us, to be aware of so much more than now. As a traditioned people, mindful of our inheritances, we live futurally, looking for kingdom come. On the other hand, we always live in the present. Past gifts and future hopes coalesce in us in the present. I can't not be now. The challenge is to faithfully inhabit the present without caving to a present-*ism* in which only now matters (the recipe for indulgent Epicureanism). The trick is to live fully present to the moment without being defined by the *Zeitgeist*.

I say "trick" but perhaps I mean "feat," in the spirit of Kierkegaard's knight of faith who is such a ballet master that he can make the stunning leap of faith seem effortless. The knights of infinite resignation, he says, leap into eternity but never figure out how to land in the world in which they find themselves: "Every time they come down, they are unable to assume the posture immediately, they waver for a moment, and this wavering shows that they are aliens in the world." There are lots of religious people for whom their faith amounts to a leap into a nostalgic past or an escapist future, but the present bedevils them: awkward and unsettled, they stumble and waver. They know how to be faithful anywhere but now. "But to be able to come down in such a way that instantaneously one seems to stand to walk, to change the leap into life into walking, absolutely to express the sublime in the pedestrian—only that knight [of faith] can do it, and this is the one and only marvel."[6] To know how to dance in divine time and walk like a human being is a marvel.

The creation that is our home, the incubator of now, is dynamic. Creation's being is becoming. Eden is already roiling with change. Ephemerality is not something that befalls creation; it is a feature of finitude. Aging is not a curse; autumn is not a punishment; not all that is fleeting should be counted loss. The coming-to-be and passing-away that characterizes our mortal life are simply the rhythms of creaturehood. There is no way of being a creature that is not subject to the vicissitudes of time. Even resurrected bodies change.[7]

In his reflections on time in the *Confessions*, St. Augustine says that my very self is the present nexus of past and future. He ventures that neither the future nor the past really exists, technically speaking. "Perhaps it would be exact to say: there are three times, a present of things past, a present of things present, a present of things to come. In the soul there are these three aspects of time, and I do not see them anywhere else."[8] Augustine, quite audaciously, suggests that the present is all there is. Which is why ephemerality is constitutive of creation. Augustine's examples often invoke speech or song as a case study for how being human requires getting used to this flow of arrival and loss.

> Suppose I am about to recite a psalm which I know. Before I begin, my expectation is directed towards the whole. But when I

> have begun, the verses from it which I take into the past become the object of my memory. The life of this act of mine is stretched two ways, into my memory because of the words I have already said and into my expectation because of those which I am about to say. But my attention is on what is present: by that the future is transferred to become the past.[9]

When I do something as simple as speak, human consciousness is a turbine of the present: drawing in the future, to speak in the now, with what has been said in my wake as past. Every conversation is a churn of anticipation and retention. "A person singing or listening to a song he knows well," Augustine continues, "suffers a distension or stretching in feeling and in sense-perception from the expectation of future sounds and the memory of past sound."[10] There is no joy in music without the fugitive nature of sound; there is no delight in the song without the gift of ephemeral notes that rise, linger, then fade to make way for more.[11]

To embrace the ephemeral is to live with such flux, to live gratefully amid change, which is just to say: to live *as* a mortal. Here might be the deep lesson of the Teacher's wisdom in Ecclesiastes: to not bemoan our mortal estate but to face it, accept it, and find rhythms in sync with the fleeting nature of time. One might say it is an exercise in redeeming vanity. "Enjoy life with the wife whom you love," the Teacher counsels, "all the days of your vain life that are given you under the sun, because that is your portion in life and in your toil at which you toil under the sun" (Eccles. 9:9). The sticky words here, "vanity" and "toil," are demoralizing and sit uneasily with the Teacher's opening injunction: "Enjoy!" Enjoy vanity, emptiness, meaninglessness?

Theologian Peter Leithart explains our confusion: The Hebrew word translated "vanity," *hebel*—sometimes even ("absurdly," Leithart remarks) "meaninglessness"—means more literally "mist" or "vapor." "When the word is used metaphorically," Leithart clarifies, "it emphasizes the ephemerality and elusiveness of human existence. Human life is *hebel* (Pss. 39:4–11; 78:33; Job 7:16) because it is impermanent, because we change and ultimately die." When the Teacher describes "everything" as *hebel* (Eccles. 1:2), "he's not saying that everything is meaningless or pointless. He's highlighting the elusiveness of the world, which slips through our fingers and escapes all our efforts to manage it." Human life is *hebel* because we are mortals: a human lifetime is like a mist that enchants us but then dissolves too quickly, a vapor that dissipates. Leithart notes that Hebel "is the name of Adam's second son, the first human to suffer death, the first to know the reality of life's vaporousness (Gen. 4.2). In the end, every last one of us is Abel (*hebel*)." The Teacher is counseling us not to resent that reality but to face it. He doesn't despair that life is like "chasing after wind" (Eccles. 1:14); rather, as Leithart points out, the Hebrew phrase should be translated "shepherding the wind."[12] This is not a counsel of despair or resignation but rather an invitation to reframe expectations such that I can "enjoy" what's before me, who is with me, fleeting as their presence might be. The question isn't whether we can escape this condition but how we will receive our mortality, how we will shepherd what's fleeting *yet given*. When my wife, as she often does, places on my desk a tiny vase of asters and zinnias, should I resent the fact they won't last forever? That their scent will fade, their petals will be litter in a few days? Should I mourn their impermanence? Or should I shepherd what I can't control by gratefully receiving them, nourishing them as long as I can, dwelling with their beauty in the now in which they're given?

What if enjoying mortality means we stop chasing the wind and learn how to hoist a sail?

The writer Robert Hudson attests that it was a quirky old poem—"The Fly" by William Oldys—that taught him how to make friends with mortality.

> The poem taught me an incomparable, paradoxical lesson, which turns out to be a key to nearly all art at all times and in all places: that which weighs us down also lifts us up. It is the key to the Psalms and Dante's *Divine Comedy* and Shakespeare's sonnets and Mozart's *Requiem* and Van Gogh's paintings. It is the lesson that centuries of Japanese poets taught with their countless haiku about cherry blossoms. The Japanese term for it is *mono no aware*, "a sense of beauty intensified by recognition of temporality." I have no doubt this is why God gave us art—to cope with the mystery of our mortality, to make sense of the fact that each life comes stamped with an expiration date. Or is mortality itself the gift because it adds such richness to life?[13]

This Japanese aesthetic principle offers insight into a creaturely embrace of ephemerality. An awareness of transience does not have to translate into melancholy lament (though perhaps in a fallen, broken world, such melancholy and mourning is always just under the surface and will understandably break through). An awareness of transience can deepen appreciation and gratitude. Indeed, for Yoshida Kenkō, a Japanese Buddhist monk from the fourteenth century, fleetingness illumines and accentuates beauty. "If man were never to fade away like the dews of Adashino, never to vanish like the smoke over Toribeyama, how things would lose their power to move us!"[14] The intense beauty of the cherry blossoms is haloed by the short life of each bloom. What is required here is a specific kind of attention. Thus Abutsu-ni, a Japanese nun from the thirteenth century, counseled poets to, above all, pay attention: "They must know *mono no aware*, 'Ah-ness of things'—sensitivity and the ability to perceive things as they are—and keep their mind clear. They must notice and keep their heart alert to the scattering of flowers, the falling of leaves, dew and showers, and when the leaves change color."[15] A sensitivity to the "Ah-ness of things": that, it seems to me, is the way to enjoy even what is transitory.

• • •

I think Hudson is right: artists help us best appreciate this fragile dynamism of creaturehood. This is no doubt true because art specializes in ambiguity and nuance. What is art but the practiced discipline of evoking but not pinning down? A film, a poem, a song can invite us into multiple states of mind, evoking conflicting emotions yet managing to hold them together so that we dwell in the world with an unspoken appreciation for its messiness and a newfound humility in the face of its complexity. Our mortality is fraught and the arts are a balm, not because they heal us of our mortality but because they absolve us of the need to control, to fix, to escape. Like the poetry of Ecclesiastes, they give us words and images that honor the entanglement we experience as creatures.

Our mortality is fraught—enjoyment and toil are companions—because we experience so much loss that is tragic and that ought not to be. What we experience is not *just* mortality and creaturehood but its postlapsarian variety ruined by sin, a world that is not *just* temporal but a temporality in which the Fall has wreaked havoc. It becomes difficult to sift tragedy from good, creaturely rhythms in which even good things fade. Because mortality in this fallen world is so bound up with wrenching heartbreak, we come to resent mortality itself. All decay seems like disaster.

But to dwell mortally is to achieve a way of being in the world for which not all change is loss and not all loss is tragic—while at the same time naming and lamenting those losses that ought not to be. Like Kierkegaard's ballet dancer, we are back on that tightrope. To be faithfully mortal is a feat of receiving and letting go, celebrating and lamenting. Being mortal is the art of living with loss, knowing when to say thank you and when to curse the darkness.

Elizabeth Bishop's masterful poem "One Art" is a meditation on just this precarious act.

> The art of losing isn't hard to master;
> so many things seem filled with the intent
> to be lost that their loss is no disaster.
>
> Lose something every day. Accept the fluster
> of lost door keys, the hour badly spent.
> The art of losing isn't hard to master.
>
> Then practice losing farther, losing faster:
> places, and names, and where it was you meant
> to travel. None of these will bring disaster.
>
> I lost my mother's watch. And look! my last, or
> next-to-last, of three loved houses went.
> The art of losing isn't hard to master.
>
> I lost two cities, lovely ones. And, vaster,
> some realms I owned, two rivers, a continent.
> I miss them, but it wasn't a disaster.
>
> —Even losing you (the joking voice, a gesture
> I love) I shan't have lied. It's evident
> the art of losing's not too hard to master
> though it may look like (*Write* it!) like disaster.[16]

Some things, the poet observes, seem intent on being lost, made for their demise ("planned obsolescence," as Silicon Valley puts it). These things have an arc of existence, and we shouldn't be surprised by their twilight fade to black. Still, there's an art to losing. One has to learn how to lose: to see the signs of what's made to be temporary, to enjoy without clinging and clasping, so that when such things are gone it's not a disaster. There is a lightness of touch to this poem, a wit and humor, that feels a bit like trying to talk oneself into this posture. The grin and chuckle feel like a nervous attempt to fake it till we make it.

The losses accumulate—which is to say, we have lots of opportunity to practice this art. We can imagine learning to lose car keys and such. We tell ourselves losing a watch shouldn't matter, except that it's mother's watch and it's easy for us to imagine an aura around it that is about so much more than the material. Not a disaster, but not easy either.

The losses keep mounting, which is just to say: the poet continues living.[17] There is deepening ache to later losses, even if they, too, should be expected. There will always be a last visit to a beloved city or hometown, a last foray to the contemplative sanctum of the Montana wilderness, a final adventure in Europe, the last time you'll walk over the Pont de Notre-Dame and be quietly mesmerized by the cathedral that bears the scars of its own combustibility.

And then the loss we're dreading, the loss we know is coming: "you." Every one of us imagines someone in that line. There is an art even to losing you, and the poet doesn't want to lie: it should be possible. But here is the written testament, a protest bearing on refusal, that this certainly looks like disaster.

A young Augustine experienced this sort of disaster, an experience of loss where we lose our stars and the entire cosmos dims to a jaded meaninglessness. But looking back, the older Augustine would say that his younger self hadn't yet learned the art of losing and hadn't yet imagined how loss is reframed by resurrection. "'Happy is the person who loves you,'" Augustine prays, "and his friend in you, and his enemy because of you.

Though left alone, he loses none dear to him; for all are dear in the one who cannot be lost."[18] The art of losing is not easy; for mortals, it amounts to an acrobatic feat on the tightrope; but we practice above the net of the God who is all in all.

• • •

One more vignette from the arts, as glimpses of the art of losing gratefully, the dance of dwelling mortally. In a vulnerable memoir in which he tries to make sense of both his doubt and the faith that won't let him go, the poet John Terpstra often finds himself surprised not only to be in church but to long for it. "This is the only place I know where time and eternity meet on a regular basis," he confesses. No small part of this, he says, is the *singing* (which, as Augustine already pointed out, is an art of ephemerality in itself). "Where else do you sing with a group of people?" he asks. "The singing, especially in harmony, does something physical. It fills the head as though it were a chamber, a cathedral. It causes sympathetic vibrations in the veins and arteries that stretch across the stringed instruments of the body. It resonates in the body." The parishioner singing out of tune, somehow, strangely, only deepens the experience.[19]

Perhaps it is fitting, given Augustine's reflections, that the ephemerality of sound becomes, nevertheless, a chamber in which to meet mortality. "A few years after we began coming to St. Cuthbert's," Terpstra recalls, "someone rose during the service and sang Handel's 'And the Dead Shall Be Raised Incorruptible.'"

> The title of the music alone had me thinking about my three brothers-in-law, who had died fifteen years earlier, in their late teens and early twenties, within six months of each other, of the disease muscular dystrophy, with which they were born.

> And something happened. The singer was suffering from a cold that day, and had trouble reaching some of the high notes. But the un-reached notes began to meld with the brothers' short lives, which they had lived to the full, and with thoughts of their bodies, corrupted by disease, until it seemed clear that the singing suited their memory, and the music, more truly than if every note had been hit dead on.[20]

Not all change is loss, and not all loss is tragic, but some loss is tragic. This is why hope is entwined with lament, and even our resurrection songs are sung with voices that crack and break.

• • •

I opened this book recounting a season of debilitating depression. I spent months, years, in a malaise that devoured my will to live before the gift of a counselor who helped me climb out of that pit. More recently, when it felt like the light could once again be eclipsed by that dark sun, my wife helped me to note a connection that might have been a trigger. "I don't think you've ever noticed," she gently pointed out, "that your depression set in when we moved to this house." She was recalling our move from our first house to our current home ten years ago. We lived for a decade in a humble, cozy house on Baldwin Street. It was the first house we'd ever owned, the house in which we raised our kids from children to teens, even if it felt increasingly small as they grew into their gangly selves. It was a house into which we poured our sweat and tears, tearing down walls, carving out a makeshift rec room in the Michigan basement where I created a reading nook for the kids to curl up with their Harry Potter books. It was the house where our dear neighbors, Sue and Melissa, audaciously surprised us after one spring break and we came home to refinished hardwood floors. It was the house where we learned how to live in a city, the joys of a mixed-use neighborhood, the riches and challenges of a diverse community.

In the very instant she suggested it, I knew that Deanna was right. Having lived through a traumatic displacement in my childhood, my body kept score. This loss is one of the things I carry. Of course there were a thousand important differences! We weren't being torn from a home; we were choosing to move to a beautiful new house where our kids could blossom and we could show hospitality. Our move wasn't bound up with the dissolution of a family. But nobody told my body; nobody informed my gut; nobody sat down with the heartbroken child I carried in my soul for whom moving meant tragedy—an ending. I can see now, with almost a decade of retrospect and the gift of a good counselor: moving houses tore open a wound.

I hadn't yet learned that not all change is loss, and not all loss is tragic. I hadn't yet learned the art of losing. The only repertoire I had available was the not-so-subtle art of imploding. Deanna, I now see, was inviting us to practice a different art. On the day we handed over the keys to a new owner, Deanna guided all of us, the entire family, room by room, to remember with gratitude, to recall shared delights and struggles, to relive the parties and sleepovers. Room by room we practiced an art of losing that received without grasping. Not all change is loss; not all loss is tragic.

A couple of years later, our daughter defied our then-parental restriction on tattoos. But she knew the way to our hearts. She unveiled the tattoo and explained the litany of numbers on her arm: the coordinates for that house on Baldwin Street, the house that built her.

In one of his earliest works, called *Of True Religion*, Augustine begins to address what will be an enduring theme across his corpus for the rest of his life: how to love. "Space offers us something to love, but time steals away what we love and leaves in the soul crowds of phantasms which incite desire for this or that. Thus the mind becomes restless and unhappy, vainly trying to hold that by which it is held captive. It is summoned to stillness so that it may not love the things which cannot be loved without toil."[21] The trick, Augustine says, is to learn to love what you'll lose. That doesn't mean despising what can't endure or hating what is transitory. It means holding it with an open hand, loving it in the ways appropriate to mortal things. When love is rightly ordered, we can embrace even the ephemeral.

## MEDITATION 3

# ECCLESIASTES 11:7–12:8

[7] Light is sweet, and it is pleasant for the eyes to see the sun.
[8] Even those who live many years should rejoice in them all; yet let them remember that the days of darkness will be many. All that comes is vanity.
[9] Rejoice, young man, while you are young, and let your heart cheer you in the days of your youth. Follow the inclination of your heart and the desire of your eyes, but know that for all these things God will bring you into judgment.
[10] Banish anxiety from your mind, and put away pain from your body; for youth and the dawn of life are vanity.
[12:1] Remember your creator in the days of your youth, before the days of trouble come, and the years draw near when you will say, "I have no pleasure in them"; [2] before the sun and the light and the moon and the stars are darkened and the clouds return with the rain; [3] in the day when the guards of the house tremble, and the strong men are bent, and the women who grind cease working because they are few, and those who look through the windows see dimly; [4] when the doors on the street are shut, and the sound of the grinding is low, and one rises up at the sound of a bird, and all the daughters of song are brought low; [5] when one is afraid of heights, and terrors are in the road; the almond tree blossoms, the grasshopper drags itself along and desire fails; because all must go to their eternal home, and the mourners will go about the streets; [6] before the silver cord is snapped, and the golden bowl is broken, and the pitcher is broken at the fountain, and the wheel broken at the cistern, [7] and the dust returns to the earth as it was, and the breath returns to God who gave it. [8] Vanity of vanities, says the Teacher; all is vanity.

The Teacher, it turns out, is a poet. This concluding counsel is a lyrical musing from the twilight of a life. The world-weariness is palpable but hard-earned. But it is penned in hope. Indeed, the very act of bequeathing wisdom to the next generation is a defiance of despair, an act that transcends the transitoriness to which the Teacher attends. All is vapor. And yet here we are reading the ancient text of Ecclesiastes in the twenty-first century.

It's easy to imagine this as a voice-over in a Terrence Malick movie. You can hear an aged Jim Caviezel or a grizzled Matthew McConaughey narrating scenes of shimmering light and roiling dark clouds, curtains blowing in the breeze of abandoned rooms, and time-lapsed miracles of almond trees blooming, yielding, falling. And faces: some smiling, some pleading; eyes closed under the warmth of the sun, eyes weeping in the dark; faces downcast and faces turned to the sky, radiant and expectant. The faces of the Teacher's life flashing past him. In a way, the Teacher is inviting his student to a kind of time travel: heed my words, listen to what I've learned in this long life, and you will know in advance what I only discovered after the fact. Learn from the arc of my life and you'll be able to "remember" what you haven't yet experienced. I suspect the Teacher is old enough to know that, sadly, youth is rarely primed to receive such a gift.

To look at a life from its end has a winnowing effect. Certain simple joys crystallize, like the faithful reappearance of the sun and the way it rekindles possibility. Those who have lived many years have circled this source of light many times, and each year is a cause for joy, says the Teacher. But such a life also endures many nights. *Hello darkness, my old friend*.

This poetic conclusion hovers between "vanity" and gratitude. Or not exactly *between* but rather gratitude *in the midst of* vanity, even gratitude for what is *hebel*. Let us remember that "vanity" is not our best translation here; all life is a *vapor*, the Teacher reminds us. All that's coming, young man, is vapor. That doesn't mean life is empty or meaningless; it's just that our lives are fleeting, ephemeral, fugitive, given to rhythms of consolidation and dissolution. Like a mist that evaporates, not only does our mortal life come to an end, but the seasons and microepochs that make up our lifetime coalesce and form like clouds that appear solid and formidable, only to disappear in the afternoon.

And yet even in the vapor are good gifts. The Teacher is not Albert Camus, who counsels us to act *as if*, to make meaning where there is none, to be Sisyphus and yet, in spite of everything, resolve to be happy. The Teacher's wisdom is different: life is not meaningless; it is just brief, tenuous, liquid, melting away, hard to hold on to. Embodied spirits like us live on breath; vapor is living water too. Inhale, the Teacher says.

So rejoice, you young, while you are young. *Be* young, even though it's hard to understand youth until you've lost it. (And you elders: remember what you wasted and grant the youth what you now long for.) Remember *whose* you are, as creatures who bear the image of your Creator, creatures whose very fleeting breath is given. Get rambunctious in your creaturehood while you have the energy and dreams and distinct joy of youth.

Wisdom, says the Teacher, is an awareness of why *when* matters. This passage is littered with seasonal phrases ("the days of your youth") and temporal markers like "before" and "while" and "when." When you understand that life is a vapor and appreciate that the seasons of life are both expected and transitory, you're primed to inhabit them with the proper expectations: to know when you are and dwell in that now, but in such a way that you recognize this too shall pass. To be so temporally attuned enables one to recognize the eras and epochs in which we find ourselves—"the days when" our collective conditions have shifted and the strong men are bent and the women who labor are weary and "all the daughters of song are brought low" (12:4). To face such times without the delusion of American can-do-ism or some cheery, pious spin. To not be surprised by the seasons when desire fails and mourning is the order of the day, when all the vessels that hold water are broken and we are ever so thirsty. To walk into the fog of those seasons when we see dimly through every window and to not imagine that God has left us, because even the vapor is the Lord's.

# 5

# SEASONS OF THE HEART

*How to Inhabit Your Now*

> For everything there is a season, and a time for every matter under heaven.
>
> —Ecclesiastes 3:1

We experience seasons because the earth is askew. While the planet orbits the sun on a level plane, it leans 23.5 degrees from the plane of that ecliptic—a curious reality you might recall from the globe in your sixth-grade science class. As the earth makes its way around the sun, the tilt in its orbital axis means that at one end of the orbit, the earth leans away from the sun; at the other end of its orbit—six months later—it leans toward the sun.

This cosmic geometry gives us summer and winter, spring and fall. The angle of our annual journey around the sun also makes our hemispheric location matter. When, on that one end of the orbit, the earth is leaning away from the sun, those of us in the northern hemisphere feel the chill of winter and the distance from the sun that shortens our days. But that's precisely when our neighbors in the southern hemisphere experience the closeness of that burning ball of gas that grants the delights of summer. For the three months we're approaching that end of our orbit, we begin to feel the different slant of light that is autumn, the crispness of mornings that signals winter is coming. Our bodies know the difference between a 50°F morning in March versus September because we have a keen sense of what's coming.

At the extremes, both poles and the equator, the differences are stark and seasons tend to resolve into just two. At the equator, the tilt makes little difference and the seasons are distinguished less by temperature and more by precipitation: dry and wet. But at the poles, the two seasons are almost the equivalent of two unthinkably long "days": in summer, the sun remains above the horizon for pretty much six months; in winter, it disappears for just as long—a six-month "day" that is only night.

What truly distinguishes the seasons is not distance but the availability of sunlight. What defines summer is not just the length of a day but also the concentration of the sun's energy on the earth's surface. In winter, when the sun is lower in the sky, its rays arrive at an oblique angle and the same energy is diffused, spread out, as it were, less intense. In summer, when the sun is high in the sky, light arrives more directly and thus carries an energy that makes miracles possible: seeds sprouting into zinnias, dormant tubers erupting to give us dahlias, tiny tomato blossoms eventually becoming ripe fruit. The same sun shines on us in our moderate climes all year, but only the light of summer grants the harvest of autumn. Corn for cattle is picked from withered stalks. Potatoes are forked from the earth in the cold autumn air. There is a strange irony to the fact that our bountiful harvest is plucked from gardens and fields that are dying. The gifts arrive at the end.

• • •

Chef Alice Waters founded her famous Berkeley restaurant, Chez Panisse, on a principled conviction that our relationship to food should be an intimate way of relating to the earth that yields it. The way we eat should remind us of our dependence on the earth and our embeddedness in an environment. At the time, Chez Panisse was something of an avant-garde expression of what we now know as farm-to-table dining that focuses on local ingredients, organically farmed in sustainable ways, making our plates the end of a food production chain that is attentive to the needs of both the earth itself and the future generations that will depend on it.

In her recent slow food manifesto, *We Are What We Eat*, Waters articulates the core principles of such a relationship to eating, a credo for intimacy between eaters and the earth. She contrasts this with the often unarticulated but nonetheless influential principles of fast food culture that has so forcefully, if covertly, shaped our global relationship to food and hence the globe itself. Fast food culture is not just scarfing down burgers from drive-thru windows. It is a broader set of forces that privilege convenience, uniformity, availability, and speed. These forces stand in contrast to principles of sustainable eating—what she's calling slow food culture—like biodiversity, stewardship, simplicity, and interconnectedness.

One of the key principles of slow food culture is *seasonality*. This stands in contrast to fast food culture's fixation on *availability*. Fast food culture is driven by its own kind of atemporal idealism that floats above the realities of time—it contrives a "nowhen" by making everything available everywhere, all the time.[1] "We have been conditioned to expect the endless bounty of summer foods through every season, even though that's simply not how nature works."[2] This fabricated fiction that makes me live as if it's always strawberry season both warps my expectations and undermines my attunement to the goods of the world. "When all year long you eat those same second-rate fruits and vegetables that have been flown in from the other side of the world or grown in industrial greenhouses, you can't actually see them for what they are when they come into season, when they're ripe and delicious. By that time, you're already bored."[3] When our senses are dulled by a manufactured availability, we lose our ability to taste, to judge, to discern.

We might think that giving up on perpetual availability entails loss. But Waters suggests we actually gain: "Letting go of this constant availability doesn't have to be restrictive," she argues. "On the contrary. It's about letting go of mediocrity. It is liberating."[4] When our tastes have acclimated to poor substitutes always available, we become more anxious about scarcity and less discerning about taste. Trading *availability* for *seasonality* seems scary. But Waters recounts her own epiphany: "The truth was, seasonality was an invisible force out there that we were grappling with every day, but we weren't fully committed to understanding what it meant. At a certain point, instead of being limited by seasonality, we started to embrace it."[5] And what did they find? "Understanding the seasons teaches us patience and discernment and helps us determine where we are in time and space and how we can live in harmony with nature."[6] There are spiritual analogies to work out here.

Waters adds something of a coda that also speaks to the seasonality of a life: "It is possible to eat seasonally in seemingly inhospitable climates." Critics often point out that Chez Panisse enjoys the benefits of a Mediterranean climate whose growing season is long and generous. What are the prospects for eating seasonally in Red Deer, Alberta, or Trondheim, Norway? Waters addresses the skeptics by reminding them of an ancient culinary technology: preservation. "We are so unaccustomed to eating in season that we've forgotten the traditional ways people have preserved and cooked food. I am amazed by all the ways it is possible to capture seasonality: salting cod, curing ham, pickling cabbage or carrots or turnips, canning tomatoes."[7] Sometimes seasonality means living off our preserves. Which also means living in a way that stocks for the future. One of my Bible teachers once told us, in what sounds like wisdom from Ecclesiastes: "Remember in the darkness what you learned in the light." Store up while the garden gives to survive the winter ahead. Because, dear friend, a winter is coming.

• • •

In May and June, my hands are dirty and I spend a lot of time thinking about sanctification.

After the danger of Michigan frost is past, usually after Mother's Day, we return to Hillcrest Community Garden here in Grand Rapids. It always feels like emerging from a winter cocoon. Planting is making a promise to stay near. Only care and attention will coax out the remarkable potential latent in these tiny orbs we call "seeds." The garden keeps us placed, obligated to this patch of earth.

I'm really more of a *sous* gardener; Deanna is the master. Thanks to her patient instruction, I have grown in my horticultural abilities over the past decade. For example, in the past couple of years, I've finally become able to distinguish plants from weeds. As you might imagine, the inability to do so is rather disastrous. Sometimes while aggressively fending off invaders, I uprooted the tender shoots of plants just emerging. In other cases, my ignorance meant I left weeds to flourish, choking out what we planted. Can you see why I keep thinking about sanctification?

There is something focal about weeding. Often as I have my head down, focused on a square of garden between the peppers and eggplant, my fingers plunged into the soil, my mind wanders into metaphors I learned from parables and I'm thinking about the state of my soul.

I'll start musing, for example, on the fact that the same conditions that cause our tomatoes to grow also help weeds to flourish. As long as there is a garden, there are weeds. If planting seeds is a promise to stay near, the hope of a harvest means a commitment to be here each night, weeding in the evening light while killdeers chirp and run, from May to September. Get used to it.

This year I've been thinking a lot about how tenacious the weeds can be. As I carefully pluck weeds from between the fledgling emergence of corn or carrots, I dig my fingers into the muddy clay, probing under the surface, aiming to get to the root. Too often I have to dig and dig, and by the time I'm able to yank out the root, it might be half the length of my forearm. Why, O Lord, must the weeds be so obstinate, the plants so vulnerable? Must the roots of those unwanted weeds plunge so deep, when the fruit I want to grow is so fragile? Is there no end to this weeding?

Of course, I'm speaking of a mystery: the garden that is the human heart.

Gardening has transformed the way we inhabit time. It's like a different rhythm of expectation and obligation overlays the other calendars in our lives: academic, liturgical, Gregorian. February is no longer just the doldrums of winter when the gray of west Michigan is most oppressive; it is also the month the seed catalogs arrive and Deanna begins planning for May. February is transformed into anticipation. March and April are the season of planting seeds on a heated mat under the warmth of lamps in the basement furnace room, getting a leg up on spring. This is a season of dreaming of what new, exotic seeds hold in store. It is also the beginning of being tethered: these vulnerable creatures in their tiny squares of earth need daily care. We're not going anywhere for six weeks.

In northern climes like Michigan (we hover between growing zones 5 and 6), the bulk of planting at Hillcrest Community Garden happens after Memorial Day. The clean, tilled patch of earth awaiting seeds and plants is a field of possibility: the joy of planting is rivaled only by the satisfaction of harvest. In between is the long slog of what I think of as agricultural "ordinary time," the season of weeding and watering, when we are hyperattuned to clouds and weather reports and battling the onslaught of invaders like wild parsley and ragweed. There is an incessantness to this window of time, all labor with only long-term return. We've been doing this for a decade. There's nothing surprising. To plant a garden is to sign up for this. It is what we endure for the sake of the harvest.

I guess what I mean is that gardening, with all of its micro-seasons within seasons, has attuned me to seasonality—the way time is lived in windows, chunks of history within parentheses. Life itself is epochal even if the scale is simply *my* life, which is hardly epic. Seasonality means that, rather than being governed by the unceasing ticks of a minute hand, our lives unfold in *eras*. While minutes, days, and years carve up and measure the cosmic time of Earth's course around a dwarf star, for temporal creatures like us, the *season* is perhaps the most natural form of timekeeping. The answer to the question "When am I?" isn't six o'clock or 2022; it is more like youth, middle age, chapter 3 of a life. The same is true collectively and communally, whether a marriage, an institution, or even a nation. To ask "When are we?" isn't a question of counting years as much as discerning a season, knowing what to expect, remembering that, in every season, we revolve around the Son.

• • •

The Teacher of Ecclesiastes, who is almost brutally focused on what it means to be mortal, recognizes the seasonality of creaturely time:

> For everything there is a season, and a time for every matter under heaven:
>
> a time to be born, and a time to die;
> a time to plant, and a time to pluck up what is planted;
> a time to kill, and a time to heal;
> a time to break down, and a time to build up;
> a time to weep, and a time to laugh;
> a time to mourn, and a time to dance;
> a time to throw away stones, and a time to gather stones together;
> a time to embrace, and a time to refrain from embracing;
> a time to seek, and a time to lose;
> a time to keep, and a time to throw away;
> a time to tear, and a time to sew;
> a time to keep silence, and a time to speak;
> a time to love, and a time to hate;
> a time for war, and a time for peace. (Eccles. 3:1–8)

The Teacher's poetic compilation of life's range of episodes—immortalized in popular culture by Pete Seeger's song "Turn! Turn! Turn!," most famously performed by the Byrds—conveys a sense of ineluctability. A life lived "under the sun" should expect birth and death, mourning and dancing, war and peace the same way we expect spring and fall, summer and winter. There is a predictability, even inevitability, to such times. An existential equilibrium can be found for the one who is not surprised by the arrival of such times and seasons. If we can cultivate a sense of expectation, we won't be unmoored by a season of weeping; we won't expect perpetual dancing; we could even be primed to ask ourselves, "Is this my time to die?" and thus receive even that season with a graced equanimity.

When the Teacher assigns seasonality to these moments, he is exhorting us to recognize that such experiences take time. These are episodes of duration rather than punctiliar events. Birth is not just a day but a season—the time of expecting, the ordeal of delivery, the ensuing months of a family's reconfiguration of habits, and a body's reconstitution. When I look back on our own lives with four children, each two years apart, in some ways the "time" of birth was ten years long. While we were given the obligatory copy of *What to Expect When You're Expecting*, somehow nobody told us to expect this season of travail and endurance to last for years. We didn't properly imagine that we were entering a chapter of our marriage that would last a decade. No one had taught us to expect the reverberations of trauma on a mother's body, or named the realities of postpartum depression (it was the 1990s), or spoken candidly about the challenges of physical intimacy and how that would create distance and tension even as we needed to be partners in child-rearing. Looking back on those struggles for a young marriage, I hear the counsel of Ecclesiastes afresh and am convinced that if someone could have helped us recognize the season we were in, and its very seasonality, it would have transformed our expectations and efforts. The recognition would have granted its own grace to endure.

To say that our mortal lives unfold in seasons is to emphasize that experiences have their own temporal halo. Episodes tend to have a longevity, and the very capacity to experience *takes time*, in two senses: time is required for the experience to unfold, but also the experience eats up time, consumes time, can sometimes take over our lives for a time such that the season is defined by the experience, even if we still have to brush our teeth and take out the trash and pay our taxes and go to church.[8] There are times in our lives—both individually and collectively—that will be given over to what the season requires. In this sense, a season is *focal*. It requires something of us, but if we "give it time"—giving over our time to the experience, allowing it the time it needs to unfold—we also get something back: we carry something from the experience.

To say that there is a time to die and a season to mourn is to recognize that dying asks something of us and grief takes time. This insight informs the Jewish practice of sitting shiva after the death of a loved one. For seven days, mourners come to the home of the bereft to sit, traditionally sitting on low stools or boxes and hence "brought low" with those who have experienced loss. Those in mourning do not work, and those who surround them help mourn the loss in a variety of ways. The elongation of the experience by this ritual structure provides a framework for properly undertaking the work of mourning as something that must be undergone as a means of finding peace, stability, acceptance (even though the loved one will be annually remembered on Yahrzeit, the annual anniversary of their death). Sitting shiva illustrates the paradox: taking time gives back. Giving ourselves over to the season is a way to receive what we need to take from it into the next.

Letting the season take the time it demands can sometimes be grueling and doesn't immediately translate into rejuvenation. Sometimes what is required of us is to pass through a season of reckoning, including reckoning with our own (collective) sins and failures. To give ourselves over to such a season—to focus on what it demands—means not to rush to resolve it or escape but to endure, undergo, let go of what needs to be taken from us. The Teacher's counsel is like an ancient Hebrew precursor to Alice Waters: instead of being limited by seasonality, we should embrace it. "Taking the time" is a way of letting the season shape us, and ultimately there is a trust that God's providential and caring hand is not only behind the season but holding us *through* it.

If seasonality is a recognition of inevitability and duration, there is also a sense of assignation in this passage: "a time *for* every matter," "a time *to* act." If there are seasons in which we should expect certain kinds of experiences to befall us, there are also times when certain actions are expected of us. While some of these seasons arrive without our bidding (birth, death, weeping, laughing), much of what the Teacher counsels here assumes our agency. In this sense, Ecclesiastes is both teaching us what to expect and also exhorting us to recognize what's called for, what's expected *of* us in different seasons. Sometimes we are called to embrace; in other seasons we might best bear witness to justice by refusing to embrace some pseudoreconciliation. There will be times when we should be building, launching, founding; but in a transitory world, sometimes wisdom will be knowing when to shut it down and dismantle. It might be hard to imagine there could ever be a season that calls for us to tear; shouldn't we be weavers, menders, repairing the social fabric? Yes, but sometimes that will mean tearing down the flags and monuments that have functioned as barriers for full inclusion, mementos of terror that only deserve to be torn down. We will be primed to ask ourselves, "Is this a season for me to be quiet?" without fretting we'll never be heard again. (White men, I'm talking to us!)

Seasons are focal insofar as they ask something of us for a time. But that focal demand is not only passive (that we should undergo something); sometimes the season calls for us to be active and agential: we are called to *do* something "for such a time as this" (Esther 4:14 NIV).

But here the Teacher seems to leave out something crucial. While he rightly counsels us to recognize, both individually and collectively, that our lives will be lived in seasons, and to thus recognize what the times require, what he doesn't tell us is *how to know what time it is*. How do we recognize our season, whether collectively or individually? How do we know when it's the time to plant or the season to pluck up? How does a season come into focus, and how does our responsibility and calling in that season come into focus? Can we know *in the midst of it*? How?

• • •

We return again to one of the core disciplines of faithful temporal awareness: *discernment*. More art than science, discernment is an effort at orientation, and I am suggesting one of the most significant exercises of discernment we can undertake across our lives is to grasp our *seasonal* location. The challenge is that a season coalesces most often ex post facto: it's only after we've come through a "time" like Ecclesiastes describes that we recognize it as a season. This is Hegel's point when he says the owl of Minerva flies at dusk: insight tends to crystallize at the end of things.

But in order to provide wisdom for how to live, we need to discern our seasonal location while *in medias res*, in the middle of things. In this regard, discernment is more like echolocation than a God's-eye overview. We never get the luxury of being able to *transcend* our season, to rise above it and see the whole with some kind of spiritual drone. Discernment, especially *temporal* discernment, is more like being in the midst of a cornfield and achieving dead silence so that you might hear a truck's crunch on the gravel road or the faint babbling of the creek and thereby get your bearings.

Or we could say that discernment is a bit like sleep. On the one hand, we act to make ourselves available for sleep: I take up my evening ritual of reading, and when I sense sleep's descent, I quiet and darken the room; I fall into the posture of my body that I've learned is a way sleep often befalls me; I quiet my breathing, and I wait. Yet that waiting is its own activity. I have primed myself for (hopefully!) sleep's gentle arrival, a kind of daily nocturnal gift.

In the same way, discernment inhabits this space between activity and reception. In *Gaudete et exsultate*, Pope Francis's apostolic exhortation on holiness in today's world, he reminds us that discernment is ultimately the reception of a gift. Discernment, he says, "calls for something more than intelligence or common sense. It is a gift which we must implore. If we ask with confidence that the Holy Spirit grant us this gift, and then seek to develop it through prayer, reflection, reading and good counsel, then surely we will grow in this spiritual endowment."[9] Discernment requires something of us, but it is not a feat of our ingenuity; "discernment is a grace."[10] We need only to achieve the posture of receptivity to welcome it.

Every season is a season for listening, and perhaps especially listening to voices and whispers to which you haven't attended before. In this sense, discernment should be a primary, ongoing spiritual discipline of the Christian life and the Christian community. "Discernment is necessary not only at extraordinary times, when we need to resolve grave problems and make crucial decisions," Pope Francis continues. "We need it at all times, to help us recognize God's timetable, lest we fail to heed the promptings of his grace and disregard his invitation to grow. Often discernment is exercised in small and apparently irrelevant things, since greatness of spirit is manifested in simple everyday realities. It involves striving untrammeled for all that is great, better and more beautiful, while at the same time being concerned for the little things, for each day's responsibilities and commitments."[11] Discernment of season is a striving to hear our focal calling for a time, and how that focus should organize our lives for a season, even though we are still called to manage all the other quotidian commitments.

This isn't the same as mere prioritization, though it is certainly related. On a personal scale, for example, discerning one's season will often be a matter of prayerfully listening for what aspect of my multiple callings should take precedence and then living into the freedom of such focus. "Oh, OK: this is what I'm supposed to be doing *now*." That doesn't mean it won't feel like drudgery. But to give oneself over to it for a season is always accompanied by the realization it's not forever.

Many, for example, experience a long season where child-rearing is a focal calling ("This too shall pass!" counsels the empty nester). The season is a mix of terror and joy, weariness and fulfillment. It often overlaps with other crucial times in the life of parents—the early era of a marriage when we're still merging and negotiating our own family histories; times of professional aspiration; sometimes the experience of parental loss. To recognize a chunk of one's life as a season given over to child-rearing has a tempering effect on other obligations that should, in some sense, be liberating. I am reminded that I don't always have to do everything perfectly: right now, in this season, our focus is this one primal thing: to steward the lives of these vulnerable gifts into the flourishing image bearers God has entrusted to us. When you take your oldest to college, you'll start to feel the autumn of this season in the air and you'll wonder where it has gone. The season of parenting is that chunk of personal history where our children are the most proximate, embodied incarnation of the neighbor we are called to love—even if we are also called to love the neighbor who fell among thieves.

In the later chapters of a life, we might find that, whatever we might have had planned for that season, the Spirit is calling us to attend to a loved one who is ill and fading. To answer that call is to recognize a vocational focus for a time. Giving ourselves over to that might be difficult; we may also have to mourn what we had planned. "We must be willing to let go of the life we had planned," says E. M. Forster, "so as to have the life that is waiting for us."[12] To give ourselves over to the burden is to entrust ourselves to the God who calls.

Sometimes, like a boxer taking off a round, what we need to hear for a season is "Rest." This is not just the episodic respite of a vacation but a prolonged season of retreat, a time in which we are focused on rejuvenation, restoration, recharging. If we have been engaged and active (say, in public life) or if we have been caught up in the dynamics of attention that characterize our Instagrammed world, such a season of retreat might feel like withdrawal. It might, to some, look like a kind of selfishness. But that's to view a life as a snapshot rather than a video. Over the course of a life, an intentional season of pulling back, even a season of spiraling into interiority, might be precisely what we need to emerge as better servants.

In other cases, discerning a season means recognizing that one will be experiencing something for a time and giving oneself over to that. It could be that you begin to find yourself gaining attention you hadn't expected, perhaps because of a notable accomplishment—your fifteen minutes of fame might have arrived. Or it could be something much more difficult: the irruption of a family trauma or an illness introduces an inescapable suffering; a dark night of the soul; the chilled loneliness of a time when God seems not only distant but absent, even unbelievable. It may seem strange to say, but if Ecclesiastes is right, there are times to *live with* these things, to dwell with them in order to let them do their work. To recognize their seasonality is to grant them a focus for a time—to give oneself over to it—but to do so in a way that recognizes it as temporary and transitory. Go with it; don't get used to it.

This will also be true of our collective life in institutions and nations. Here the difficulty of discernment is amplified by the messiness of history with its many variables and story lines. Discernment is also more complicated when we are trying to get a handle on our collective location in time and history.[13] Yet it is surely the case that a collective *we*—whether "we the people" or "we parishioners" or "we farmers"—experience history in chunks we call "seasons."

Our recent experience of the COVID-19 pandemic might be an example. In ways we never could have anticipated, the entire world was catapulted into a shared time that, for many of us, was unprecedented. The pandemic season required things of us—a new intentionality about solidarity for the sake of public health, for example, in which, paradoxically, caring meant keeping our distance. It became a season that required new intentionality about our worship and our friendships. (In Michigan, maintaining friendships meant sitting around fires in 25°F weather, bundled in parkas, wrapped in sleeping bags.) We had to forge new habits to answer the call to community. Many also experienced this season of social distancing and isolation and psychological taxation as a season of "languishing,"[14] and so we asked ourselves afresh: What's required of us right now? Expending the energy to answer the calls of public health, many of us gave ourselves permission to relax in ways we perhaps never have before—the glorious permission to be unproductive. "It's a pandemic!" we told ourselves and one another, granting permission for a time. (Confession: I played two hundred hours of Formula 1 racing on my newly purchased

Sony PS4 during 2020. I regret nothing.) Collectively, we were all negotiating a season that was focal and demanding. Discerning it *as* a season was almost too obvious; discerning what to do *in* the season proved more challenging.

I am reminded of a stirring observation made by Apsley Cherry-Garrard on the strange gift of a summer blizzard in the Antarctic:

> The temperature, never very low, rises, and you are not cold in the tent. Sometimes a blizzard is a very welcome rest: after weeks of hard pulling, dragging yourself awake each morning, feeling as though you had only just gone to sleep, with the mental strain perhaps which work among crevasses entails, it is most pleasant to be put to bed for two or three days. You may sleep dreamlessly nearly all the time, rousing out for meals, or waking occasionally to hear from the soft warmth of your reindeer bag the deep boom of the tent flapping in the wind, or drowsily you may visit other parts of the world, while the drifting snow purrs against the green tent at your head.[15]

Sometimes it takes a blizzard to give us permission to dream. A season of being hemmed in could be a gift because we learn something about ourselves we would never have discovered in our frenetic busyness. Discernment is not some magical affirmation of whatever happens; it is an attentiveness to the gifts we might have missed.

Another example of a collective season would be the time marked by the murder of George Floyd and the way his death at the hands of police catalyzed a season of collective reckoning with systemic racism—a season we are very much still in.[16] Many recognized this as a time to uproot bias and break down barriers; a time for white people who enjoy power and privilege to take stock of not just their personal prejudices but also their implication in systems that have benefited them and intentionally marginalized, excluded, and oppressed Black people; a time for a white majority to listen and a Black minority to speak. To *embrace* seasonality, as Alice Waters put it, is to dwell intentionally with what the times require of us—to neither hasten nor delay but rather listen, attend, undergo, reckon. This season cannot pass as long as injustice endures.

• • •

We will learn to embrace seasonality only if we cultivate the gift of discernment. It is discernment that enables us to grasp what season we're in, what that season requires of us, and what we might need from it. To embrace seasonality is to cultivate an availability to the moment, entrusting ourselves to the Lord of history and willing to live through the mystery that is time. This requires a special kind of patience that is a willingness to not judge a zig until we've lived through the zag, so to speak—to wait for the season to unfold before resenting what it's taken. Sometimes the gifts come at the end.

This posture of discernment, I've emphasized, requires prayerful listening in the midst of things, since we never get to be above the fray, looking at our now from a nowhen. However, there is one way to almost cheat and get outside your now. If you want to transcend time, build friendships across generations. Though you can't stand outside your season, you can hear from those who've lived through such seasons. In my experience, this is one of the great gifts of multigenerational friendships.[17] Friendship, in this respect, is akin to time travel. There are patterns of a human life that, despite our claims to utter uniqueness, are in fact repeated and shared. We're never quite as special as we imagine, and so much of what humans endure and celebrate in their fourscore and seven is shared. If we can relinquish the myth of utter singularity, then listening to those generations ahead of us is a way of learning from our future. Granted, it is in the nature of youth to spurn such gifts. But when we are humbled, friendship across generations becomes a lifeline, an almost sacramental means of transcending the purview of our now as God gives us an outside glimpse of our moment.

But the gifts traverse time both ways. Older generations attentively listening to those younger avail themselves of different ears to hear what's whispering or shouting in the now. As a professor of undergraduates, I feel like every classroom is a time machine, every incoming class a new dispatch from the present that otherwise eludes me.

In my experience, so often the word that comes from older friends sounds like the gospel itself as they gently say, "Be not afraid." You might look at the life of an older friend, which seems intentional and grounded and placid, and you imagine it was a straight path. When you look at such a life from the mire in which you might find yourself—overwhelmed, failing, and flailing—it's easy to be given to both despair and envy. But then in a conversation you discover they've lived through past seasons you didn't see. You realize this friend has found this life on the other side of a season much like what you're enduring. Indeed, a conversation with such a friend might finally crystallize for you that you're *in* a season. That conversation doesn't end the difficult season, but it immediately stirs hope because now you're getting a report from the other side, which lets you know there is life beyond what presses in the now and blocks our ability to see a different future. When an older friend reports from a future you couldn't imagine, your imagination is infused with a new possibility. That's called hope.

Eventually, recognizing the season you're in means recognizing that you're the one who is now the elder, the one who has endured, the one who can come back to younger friends with wisdom wrested from your experience. Like Plato's philosopher who is compelled to return to the cave, you have an obligation to go back in time, as it were, simply by being a counselor to someone now living through an experience you've survived. Trading testimonies across generations turns the communion of saints into a time machine.

• • •

Learning from those who've gone before is particularly pertinent for the rhythm of our personal lives, in which seasons like adolescence and middle age, post-college and post-retirement life are, though not universal, still widely shared, experienced over and over again by successive generations. While each human life is a mystery, a distinct constellation of experiences as unique as a fingerprint, there is also a sense in which the shape of a life is, if not predictable, at least patterned.

This is less true, it seems to me, on the collective level. The patterns are less predictable for institutions and nations because the vectors of history are more given to surprise. Of course, there are analogies and patterns to be discerned. There are reasons why we can't stop studying the history of Rome, as it harbors insights for us in the twenty-first century. Or consider that we find ourselves in a moment in history where commentators and analysts wonder whether we are experiencing a "democratic recession," worried about what that portends for the future.[18] And while there are patterns that many companies and organizations experience, which is why we're all familiar with "founder's syndrome," institutional and national histories rarely repeat themselves. Institutions and nations are the sorts of entities that are actors *on* and *in* history in a unique way that also makes them subject to the pitches and rolls of the waves of history in a unique way. It seems there is less repeatability about such history, which means that discernment, while not exactly *de novo*, is at least much more improvisational. While every organization or company has to, at some point, work through the transition from the founder and founding generation to subsequent leadership, no company or organization in the past had to negotiate the advent of the internet or figure out the dynamics of a gig economy. While there might be lessons to learn from the church's experience enduring a global pandemic one hundred years ago, that prior case won't yield much insight into how virtual worship and broadcast technology might have indelibly affected worship. There are enduring parameters in history, but history is also a source of unfolding novelty that requires another facet of discernment, particularly at the collective level of institutions.

What is required is a particular way of attending to history, not so much because those before have experienced what we are now enduring but because we need to understand how we got here. Only if we understand when we are can we intentionally forge a future. This, too, is a theme in Pope Francis's counsel on discernment in recent years. Rooted in the conviction that "God is at work in world history," Francis urges that discernment requires a kind of apprenticeship to history. "The accumulation of human experiences throughout history is the most precious and trustworthy treasure that one generation inherits from another. Without ever forgetting divine revelation, that enlightens and gives meaning to history and to our existence."[19] He cites the wisdom of one of his predecessors, Pope (now St.) John XXIII at the beginning of the Second Vatican Council in 1962, warning against those for whom the future is only and always a story of decline: "In the current conditions of human society they are not capable of seeing anything except ruin and woe; they go around saying that in our times, compared to the past, everything is worse; and they even go as far as to behave as if they had nothing to learn from history, which is our teacher."[20] The heart of discernment is approaching history as a teacher.

One way to describe this kind of attention to history—an apprenticeship to history that makes it our teacher—is *genealogy*, not in the narrow sense of tracking a family tree but in the deeper sense of understanding the dynamics of the past that have shaped our present. Discernment is not well served by self-congratulating histories that simply narrate our founding mythologies and confirm the stories we tell ourselves. Discernment requires an attention to history that is willing to be vulnerable to what we've buried, ignored, and would rather not hear. Only when we face those facets of our history will we properly understand *when* we are and *who* we've become.

Too many of our histories are hagiographies. What discernment requires is the discipline of genealogy, and in this regard, we would do well to learn from the likes of Friedrich Nietzsche and Michel Foucault, who, in many ways, are more honest than lots of religious folks about the vagaries of being human. Genealogy, as Foucault says, "does not resemble the evolution of a species and does not map the destiny of a people." In other words, the sort of history we learn from genealogy is not a straight-line narrative of progress and advancement. "On the contrary, to follow the complex course of descent is to maintain passing events in their proper dispersion; it is to identify the accidents, the minute deviations—or conversely, the complete reversals—the errors, the false appraisals, and the faulty calculations that gave birth to those things that continue to exist and have value for us; it is to discover that truth or being do not lie at the root of what we know and what we are, but the exteriority of accidents." Even if we affirm that we live and move and have our being in the triune God, the economy of creation means that our now is shaped by such accidents, the swirling array of contingency that congeals into a life, a society, a history. Genealogy recognizes that our present rests not on some predetermined bedrock but on "an unstable assemblage of faults, fissures, and heterogeneous layers that threaten the fragile inheritor from within or underneath."[21] Such fine-grained, honest, vulnerable history that faces up to our faults and errors, the deviations and wrong turns, is the sort of collective self-examination needed for true discernment that leads to a redemptive future.

Such work can be a reckoning. But discernment for a faithful future is possible only where we are willing to undertake such genealogical labor. If seasonality requires discernment, discernment requires both an availability and openness to God's surprise, on the one hand, as well as a willingness to let ourselves be surprised by facing the histories we've buried and effaced.

• • •

We have considered how seasons are transitory yet focal. Seasons are temporary yet bequeath to us something we carry forward. Seasons ask something of us. They both take time and give something back.

There is one other aspect of seasons we should note: in important ways, seasons are environmental and involuntary. Winter's arrival is a cosmic condition; so too is our escape from it in spring. Seasons can be *expected* and are something that befall us rather than something we bring on. It is important to recognize this so we don't confuse a season with our identity, nor imagine that a season is either a reward or a punishment.

The thing about seasons is that they are tied to climate. They depend on something other than us. There is something involuntary about the experience of seasons. We can't hasten either their arrival or their end. What if we explored this notion temporally with respect to the Christian life? The seasons of a life aren't necessarily generated by my internal temperature. The seasons of a life with God aren't a measure of my success or failure.

It was a Fleet Foxes song, "I'm Not My Season," that helped me appreciate the significance of this. "Time's not what I belong to," they sing, "and I'm not the season I'm in." I am not what I'm enduring. I am not reduced to what I am experiencing. A season doesn't define me.

• • •

While God is eternal, creatures are seasonal, and thus our relationship to God is characterized by a seasonality that is natural, expected, and good. In the same way that you relate differently to a parent when you are eighteen versus forty-eight, so it is natural to relate differently to God at different points in the journey of creaturehood through time. In some ways, this might be experienced as an ebb and a flow, with varying waves of intimacy and distance, enthusiasm and struggle. When one cultivates some expectation of this, the seasons of ebb and distance need not be alarming, even if they might be difficult and puzzling. But the seasons of relating to God might also be varying dynamics of how one experiences God's presence. One might sometimes experience seasons of intense emotional connection, a kind of exuberance of the Spirit, shared in community, in which joy is the dominant note. But then one might enter a season, perhaps surprising, where God is experienced in, and as, stillness, a contemplative season in which God's covenant faithfulness is a steady state of *enduring*. If the person from the exuberant season could see the "you" in that contemplative season, it might look like a kind of distance or coolness from the outside. But that exuberant "you" doesn't yet have the capacity to comprehend the unspeakable comfort found in that contemplation to come. God's nearness looks and feels different depending on the season you're in.

You will also find that Scripture sounds different, depending on your season. Or rather, depending on the sort of season you find yourself in, you will find yourself differently attuned to the same Word you've heard a thousand times before. Part of the profundity of the Bible is the way it can give itself to us so differently across an entire life—indeed, across millennia and generations, like a never-ending, cascading waterfall whose presence is steady but whose notes and sounds are constantly different.

Talking to Ari Shapiro beside the famous "tiny desk" at NPR headquarters in DC, pianist Igor Levit reflected on the 250th anniversary of Beethoven's birth. Do we hear his music differently today? Shapiro asked. Riffing on a comment from Miles Davis, Levit offers a fascinating insight: "Musicians hear music differently, automatically, from the past because the sounds you hear outside of your home are different than the ones 50 years ago. Cars sound different . . . signals sound different." Even more so, he goes on, "the emotional environment changed. And when we change, what we hear changes for obvious reasons. So of course, we hear music differently, and the way I hear Beethoven today will change entirely in the next."[22]

There is an important spiritual insight suggested here. Because time is not flat, God doesn't always sound the same. Of course his Word endures, just as the score for Beethoven's Ninth Symphony is "set." But that doesn't mean we don't *hear* it differently, that it doesn't *mean* anew. This is why repeated listening is a gift. The scripted repetition of the Word in the lectionary and liturgical calendar enables an ongoing encounter with Scripture precisely because the same Word will be heard differently depending on when I am and when we are. God and God's Word remain the same, but the place and season in which I (and we) hear it creates new resonances, new epiphanies. This is true in a collective sense as well. History reframes hearing. How can we read the Torah after the Holocaust? asked the Jewish philosopher Emmanuel Levinas.[23] Those communities of Black Christians who endured generations of enslavement, lynching, and discrimination at the hands of those who call themselves fellow Christians will be attuned to the Scriptures in a way their oppressors are not.[24] And it took far too long for the history of biblical interpretation to become attentive to the dignity of women as image bearers of God, and hence to reconsider—to finally even *notice*—the violence against women in the Bible.[25] How might we hear the Bible afresh after #MeToo?[26] I—and we—will become attuned to the Scriptures differently when we hear from those who've experienced a different history from our own.

There will be depths and mysteries of Scripture unavailable to me *until* I have walked through different seasons. Time is a mysterious and yet necessary condition for experiencing the depths of the Bible.

The literary critic Rita Felski gives us language to understand this principle. Interested in the way art affects us, Felski talks about the uniqueness of "aesthetic time": "Not all attunement," she says, "arrives as a bolt from the blue." A work of art, whether a painting or a poem, might not immediately affect me and grab hold of my attention in a significant way. Rather than a proverbial lightning bolt that shocks my attention, Felski says we should think about such encounters in terms of "affective climate change." There is a slow transformation of my own *capacity* to receive something over time, such that a novel or a film I watched twenty years ago, perhaps that I've even encountered multiple times, at some later point *captures* me because of a gradual change *in me* over the intervening time.[27] The film or the novel remains objectively the same; what has changed over time is my own receptors, as it were. My accrued experience—including suffering and trials, accomplishments and conversions—tills the soil of my reception in new ways. A former barrier is breached; a blind spot bypassed; a song makes it through our prior defenses, and it's as if we're hearing it for the first time. Interestingly, she notes the example of someone's transformed attention to the music of Bruce Springsteen in a way that parallels my own: "Having paid no attention to Bruce Springsteen for two decades—too obvious, too mainstream—this interviewee was suddenly, inexplicably, moved to tears."[28]

Felski describes this as the time of "incubation."[29] One of the mysteries of time, and the histories we absorb as temporal creatures, is the way experience incubates a sort of receptivity we couldn't plan, new avenues of openness to the world, unexpected needs that open up in our soul. A life lived with God through time is a period of incubation in which the Spirit of God is creating the capacity in us to hear the same Word anew and to make the Word echo afresh in the new crevices in our heart.

• • •

Eventually we reach the season that will be our last. We purchase our last pair of shoes, make our last trip to Paris, see friends for a final time, experience our final spring with crocuses emerging and daffodils defiant and quaint. Not everyone, of course, is graced with the awareness of it being the last time. Not everyone gets to say goodbye gradually. But still, many do realize when they enter such a season and are either blessed or burdened with such an awareness. How to say goodbye? How to let go? How to mourn and hope at the same time?

There is a passage in Marcel Proust's *Swann's Way* that has always deeply affected me. We see again the narrator's Aunt Léonie, who has endured a sickly existence and is in her last days. The narrator has just returned from a walk with his grandfather, who expressed how much he wished Léonie could have seen the pink hawthorns she loves so much. "Yes," she replies, "someday when it's nice out, I'll take the carriage and go as far as the gate of the park." "She said it sincerely," the narrator notes, because she also knew it would never happen; "but this desire was enough for what strength remained to her; its fulfillment would have exceeded her strength."[30] She is in the autumn of her life, and in this season, desires suffice. A wish is its own pleasure. Her retreat is no less intentional than the life she has lived. Even withdrawal asks something of her. Proust sees in her seclusion an act of strength. I have never been able to shake Proust's description of this final act: "the great renunciation."

> What had begun for her—earlier, merely, than it usually happens—was the great renunciation which comes with old age as it prepares for death, wraps itself in its chrysalis, and which may be observed at the ends of lives that are at all extended, even in old lovers who have loved each other most, even between friends bound by the closest ties of mutual sympathy, who, after a certain year, stop making the necessary journey or outing to see each other, stop writing to each other and know they will not communicate again in this world. My aunt must have known perfectly well that she would not see Swann again, that she would never again leave the house, but this final seclusion must have been made fairly comfortable to her for the very reason that, in our eyes, ought to have made it more painful for her: it was that this seclusion required of her by the diminution in her strength which she could observe each day and which, making each action, each movement, a cause of fatigue, if not pain, in her eyes gave inaction, isolation, silence, the restorative and blessed sweetness of repose.[31]

6

# ON NOT LIVING AHEAD OF TIME

## *How to Sing Maranatha!*

> To those who have seen
> The Child, however dimly, however incredulously,
> The Time Being is, in a sense, the most trying time
> of all.
>
> —W. H. Auden, "For the Time Being"

My daughter and her husband recently bought a house. Watching their roller coaster of emotions in the process brought back memories of our younger selves. I could see the initial excitement of the search, the way it sparked dreams. It was like falling in love over and over again. It was so easy to imagine a future in an array of houses because they all seemed to harbor the possibility of being a home. Young love makes our hearts supple and open.

Then we watched the round of disappointments as bids were rejected, as they were outbid, as they lost out over and over again and the exhaustion set in.

Until the one that clicked, just when they'd given up, like a thief in the night. For those supple, openhearted hopes, it meant this was "the one" all along, their "meant-to-be" house. Their love will make it such.

But then that vexing season of waiting. The offer is accepted, your new reality has dawned. Wait for the inspection. Wait for the assessment. Then that curious season of escrow in which "your" house is occupied by hangers-on who seem to be squatting in your future. You're buying curtains and stockpiling paint swatches and already planning your first party. But you have to wait. You have to dwell in what Auden calls "the Time Being." The Christian life is like living in escrow: the Creator has retaken possession, but we're waiting for closing.

• • •

The philosopher David Hume noted that we can only imagine on the basis of what we have experienced. Our imagination draws on a well filled by "sense impressions," he says, which then fund our fantasy. "Nothing, at first view, may seem more unbounded than the thought of man, which not only escapes all human power and authority, but is not even restrained within the limits of nature and reality. To form monsters, and join incongruous shapes and appearances, costs the imagination no more trouble than to conceive the most natural and familiar objects."[1] We can conjure entire worlds of fantasy and fiction right inside our heads. We can dream up all kinds of fantastical creatures we've never encountered in the world, like the weird cornucopia of creatures in the Mos Eisley cantina on Tatooine. The power of human imagination seems limitless.

"But," Hume points out, "though our thought seems to possess this unbounded liberty, we shall find, upon a nearer examination, that it is really confined within very narrow limits, and that all this creative power of the mind amounts to no more than the faculty of compounding, transposing, augmenting, or diminishing the materials afforded us by the senses and experience."[2] Even our most outlandish imaginings are compositions of what we have experienced. Even our wildest dreams bear the imprint of what we have already seen.

Such limits are not losses. These are simply the constraints of creaturehood, the parameters of finitude. This limitation is why human hopes for the future are longings for a world like the one we've experienced, minus the sorrow. While God promises to exceed all that we could ask or think, God still speaks to our hope with pictures of a future world that thrums with the life of the world we know. When the prophet Isaiah pictures the world to come in Isaiah 60, he tells us of families regathered and restored (60:4), surrounding tables with abundance for all (v. 5), in a creation that sings and worships (vv. 6–7). Gone are anxieties about our borders (vv. 10–11). There is room for everyone in our cedar houses (v. 13). All are welcome, none are oppressed, and violence shall be no more (vv. 14–18). All of this is not the descent of some otherworldly reality; it is the fruit of a shoot that God has already planted in the here and now (v. 21).[3] What God's revelation invites us to imagine is a version of the world we already know renewed and transformed—recognizable, but recognizably new.

In *Arctic Dreams*, the writer Barry Lopez is wonderfully attentive to what creation wants to be. In the beautiful, difficult serenity of Arctic austerity, he describes a dignified "innocence" displayed in the patient endurance of the musk ox. Looking at a small herd of adults and calves, placid and implacable, the thought occurs to him: "They were so intensely good at being precisely what they were."[4]

In this context of contemplation, Lopez recalls a story about the world to come. A Chipewyan guide named Saltatha once asked a French priest what lay beyond the present life. "You have told me heaven is very beautiful," he said. "Now tell me one more thing. Is it more beautiful than the country of the muskoxen in the summer, when sometimes the mist blows over the lakes, and sometimes the water is blue, and the loons cry very often? That is beautiful. If heaven is still more beautiful, I will be glad. I will be content to rest there until I am very old."[5]

• • •

There is an interesting exchange, later in Augustine's life, in which he counsels Boniface, a Roman general governing the precinct of Africa at the time. Frustrated by uprisings and incursions of those who despise the Christian faith, Boniface is becoming impatient. He thinks he knows what the kingdom of God is supposed to look like, and so he is increasingly tempted to impose it—to *make* the kingdom come, as it were. But Augustine cautions him with an admonition that could shape an entire life: "We ought not to want to live ahead of time with only the saints and the righteous."[6]

This insight is at the heart of a practical eschatology and should be the shape of the Christian life. Christians are a futural people. Every day we pray for God's kingdom *to come*. But as long as we are praying it, it hasn't yet arrived, which means we are also a *waiting* people. There are significant dangers in trying to rush the kingdom, as if we could *now* live "with only the saints and the righteous." It's not just that Christians keep a different calendar; Christians keep time differently because we are citizens of a kingdom that will arrive from the future. Living eschatologically is not so much a matter of knowing the end as knowing *when* we are now. An eschatological orientation isn't only about a future expectation but also a recalibration of our present.

This peculiar time-dwelling, and hence timekeeping, of the body of Christ sets us at odds with other dominant modes of inhabiting time, including some that parade themselves as "Christian." For example, such an eschatological orientation actually sits in deep tension with escapist end-times fixation and other subtle Gnosticisms that assert a radical rift between the present and the eschaton. Such a bifurcation is almost as old as Christianity itself. You can see it starkly articulated in 2 Clement, a sermon from the end of the first century: "This age and the one that is coming are two enemies. . . . We cannot, therefore, be friends of both; we must renounce this one in order to experience that one. We think that it is better to hate the things that are here, because they are insignificant, transitory, and perishable, and to love the things that are there, which are good and imperishable."[7] This misguided school of thought remains alive and well in the twenty-first century—which is ironic since, given the two thousand years that have intervened, the eternal God clearly isn't in a rush to abolish time.

Such a posture effectively nullifies history as an arena of God's action. In this seemingly pious outlook, history is profane; eternity is holy. Clement's ancient demonization of "this age" is reprised in forms of rapture-ready Christianity, since the late nineteenth century, that are looking for the second coming as an escape pod from the vicissitudes of time. Such skewed spiritualities are fixated on a future but are not futural. They are nowhen forms of piety that fetishize an atemporal eternity. Christ's coming will efface and overcome all that has come before. Liberation theologian Gustavo Gutiérrez offers a trenchant critique of such "Christianities of the future": "One must be extremely careful not to replace a [Gnostic] Christianity of the Beyond with a Christianity of the Future; if the former tended to forget the world, the latter runs the risk of neglecting a miserable and just present and the struggle for liberation."[8] In these Christianities of the future, the God they are expecting seems to bear little interest in the present, whereas a properly eschatological orientation is rooted in the attendant conviction that "God's temple is human history."[9] What we long for is a future *for* this world that has unfolded in history and endured time with groans and cries.

For the same reasons, a futural, eschatological posture runs counter to any backward-looking nostalgia that romanticizes the retro, especially in its religious forms. While history is the arena for God's redemptive action, and while God's covenantal faithfulness across time is what fuels our hope (hence the prophets' constant appeal to the exodus), faithfulness is never synonymous with a recovery project. We are never called to turn back the clock. Appeals to God's actions in history are not invoked in a spirit of "golden-age-ism"; Eden is never celebrated as our destination. Our pilgrimage is not an Odyssean return. We are pulled toward a home we've never visited.[10] We are oriented to what is *coming*, not what has been.

A properly eschatological orientation to that future also runs counter to utopianism and dominant mythologies of progress. The futural orientation of authentic Christian timekeeping is not some Pelagian "planning." The future is not ours to engineer. The strange posture of eschatological hope is one of active receptivity, an intentional openness, a labor that, paradoxically, awaits a gift. Gutiérrez is, once again, helpful on this point: "For Jesus the Kingdom was, in the first place, a gift. Only on this basis can we understand the meaning of the active human participation in its coming; the Zealots tended to see it rather as the fruit of their own efforts." Undoing the root causes of injustice and oppression—the promise of justice in the kingdom of God—will require something more radical than any agenda we could undertake, even any revolution we might instigate. Thus Gutiérrez follows Oscar Cullmann in describing Jesus's posture as an "eschatological radicalism": a hope rooted in labor that is awaiting the advent of an upheaval, a parousia of another order, a restoration and reconciliation of all things.[11]

The philosopher Edmund Husserl, a generative thinker about the nature of time consciousness, liked to speak of the "now" as a melodious chord rather than a jumble of sound. When a melody sounds, Husserl observes, "the individual notes do not completely disappear when the stimulus or the action of the nerve excited by them comes to an end. When the new note sounds, the one just preceding it does not disappear without a trace." If that were the case, "then instead of a melody we should have a chord of simultaneous notes or rather a disharmonious jumble of sounds."[12] In order for the chord to resonate, there has to be a mysterious way in which we hold a past, present, and future in us. To hear such harmony is a feat of ear and mind that holds together a "now" that is pregnant with both memory and anticipation—like a gymnast poised on the beam. A *now* is "always essentially an edge-point in an interval of time."[13]

A life lived eschatologically is a life that holds together such a chord, which is just to say: it is a way of life that lives into a beautiful tension. An eschatological life lives on the edge, always *between*, but holds in that *between* the possibility of making music. The psalmist's perplexed question "How could we sing the Lord's song in a foreign land?" (Ps. 137:4) is also a question of time: How can we sing kingdom songs in the now? The chords will often be minor, sung with weeping. But in Christ, we are already singing in the future as well. The choir that is the body of Christ is the edge-point of history such that even the new song of Revelation (5:9; 14:3) will be a reprise. We'll sing motifs we learned in history. We'll bring chords with us into the kingdom. Socrates said that philosophy was training for death. God tells us history is training for a kingdom choir. That we are a people who can forge music is one of the mysteries of creaturehood. That we are a people who can continue to sing is one of the mysteries of incarnate grace.

• • •

To live eschatologically is not just a matter of looking toward the future. It is not simply a posture of expectation. It is to live *futurally*, to inhabit the present in such a way that the future is the beating heart of my now. To live futurally is not just to look for what comes next, like waiting for a pot to boil or like a child who hears the ice cream truck's jingle three blocks away and is waiting for it to turn the corner. Such modes of waiting put a pause on living. My present life is crowded out by what's coming. In contrast to this sort of passive expectation where my being and doing are subsumed or overwhelmed by waiting, living futurally is living in such a way that my very mode of being-in-the-world is infused with anticipation. Instead of being defined by waiting, my active life is shaped by what I hope for. I am acting now on the basis of the future. I receive myself from the future. I *am* what I am called to be.

There is an admittedly cryptic but suggestive passage in Heidegger's *Being and Time* that tries to plumb this mystery. It's worth contemplating, despite its difficulty. Recall Heidegger's sense of "thrownness" we encountered earlier: the way I find myself in the midst of a life I didn't choose, a life whose lineaments and limits are the parameters of possibility for me. In an important way, I inherit who I can be. To be is to be "indebted," as Heidegger puts it.[14]

But that's not the whole story, and later we discover that, in fact, it is not my past that defines me as much as my future. Here's how Heidegger, in his idiosyncratic language, puts it:

> As authentically futural, I *am* authentically as "*having been*." Only so far as I am futural can I *be* authentically as having been. The character of "having been" arises, in a certain way, from the future.[15]

Heidegger is onto something here—this curious, mysterious bending of time in me: my past arises from my future. What has been handed down is crystallized by anticipation of a future. What I am called to be conjures and constitutes who I have been insofar as that anticipation gathers up the possibilities thrown my way into a coherent, "authentic" life.[16] Heidegger says this is what it means to see life as a kind of "project"—the projection of a possibility that takes up my past. If, for example, later in life, I finally discern and resolve to answer the call to be a poet or a pastor, that possibility pulls together my past in a new way. All my formative experiences are now recast by this different future, and my past *becomes* something I never could have anticipated in the past. In fact, Heidegger defines this as *temporality*: that distinctly human way of being-in-the-world such that I "come back to myself" from the future.[17] "I am" because of the unity and wholeness given to me by my future.

*Being and Time*, in which this passage appears, was published in 1928. Years later, when the young Heidegger's lecture notes from 1919 to 1921 were published, we learned something fascinating: the "first drafts" of his later work on futurity are found in lectures he gave on Paul's epistles to the Thessalonians. The template of what he calls "anticipatory resoluteness"—a life shaped by futurity—was, in fact, a community living toward the parousia. In other words, the place that Heidegger learns about the *futurity* of being human is from a primal Christian community awaiting the second coming.

When the young Heidegger reads 1 Thessalonians, he notes, as we have, that the Christian community's eschatological orientation is not a countdown; it's not even a matter of "objective time." It is not "waiting" in the usual sense, he argues.

> One might think, at first: the basic comportment to the *Parousia* is a waiting, and Christian hope (*elpis*) is a special case thereof. But that is entirely false! We never get to the relational sense of the *Parousia* by merely analyzing consciousness of a future event. The structure of Christian hope, which in truth is the relational sense of the Parousia, is radically different from all expectation.[18]

The eschatological community's mode of waiting is qualitatively different because its way of being futural is "radically different." The question of Christ's coming "is not a cognitive question," Heidegger rightly observes; that is, it's not a question of information. It's not a question of whether they know the day or hour, the date of arrival. Rather, "the question is decided in dependence upon their own life."[19] The question is not whether we know what's coming, but how we live in the light of such expectation. The "question of the 'When' leads back to my comportment. How the *Parousia* stands in my life, that refers back to the enactment of life itself." Heidegger finds in 1 Thessalonians what he later unpacks in *Being and Time*: "Christian religiosity lives temporality."[20] This is why we might describe this as a *practical* (rather than "speculative") eschatology: If you believe Christ is coming, the key question isn't *When?* but *How?* The question is not *How long have we got?*

but rather *How should we live now, in light of that expectation?* How will the future shape your present? How to live in light of this future?

• • •

A "practical eschatology," as I'm calling it, is the lived wisdom of knowing when we are and hence living a harmonious life, individually and collectively, that holds together the tension of the already and not-yet as a chord. It is the chord that sounds on the edge-point of *spending time with the future* and *not living ahead of time*. But practical eschatology is not just about the soul's destiny or life after death. Eschatology is primarily about how we occupy ourselves in the now, how we live in "the Time Being" in a way that bears witness to the reality of what we pray for when we long for the kingdom to come. That is why eschatology is more political than personal. An eschatology is a theology of public life, the life we share in common in the meantime.[21] Eschatology is about how *we* live in the now, and that "we" is as wide as humanity, even if we're not all keeping time in the same way.

Imagine having a curious instrument: a temporal compass. Not a clock or a wristwatch that merely counts time but an orientation device that *locates* you in history's flow, providing orientation just as a regular compass does. The revelation of God in Christ recalibrates humanity's temporal compass, which reorients us to time.

When Augustine wrote the *City of God*, I think he was trying to invent something like this device. *City of God* is a classic exercise in temporal orientation—a ranging exploration of *when* we are in order to guide *how* we are and how we respond to the vicissitudes of history. To echo Pope John XXIII's point, Augustine is a model of someone who reads history to learn from it. The exercise is grounded in something like Gutiérrez's conviction that human history is God's temple, and Augustine is interested in the particulars—the nooks and crannies, the zigs and zags, the events and episodes of the ancient past, and the calamitous present in which he believes God's providence is at work. In all of this, Augustine believes, there is something for us not only to learn but to carry. You have to listen for the whispers, Augustine counsels, because "divine providence controls even the lowest things on the earth, producing as evidence all the thousands of beauties found not only in the bodies of living creatures but even in blades of grass."[22] This is not a puppet-master picture of providence but rather a sense of God's Spirit as the breath of all creation, infusing, inspiring, sustaining, moving.

To read history in such a way is a risky endeavor for creatures because God's providence is "a profound mystery."[23] It's risky also because it requires a degree of concretion and specificity, which means we always undertake such discernment with the constraints of a purview. We will always read history from a time and place. It can be easy to conflate "reading for providence" with an exercise in theodicy, as if trying to discern the Spirit's movements in history were the same as *justifying* that history. Trying to see where the Spirit is afoot in his moment, witnessing the waning of the Roman Empire from the shore of North Africa, Augustine's project is very specific and reflects his location: "Let us therefore proceed to inquire why God was willing that the Roman Empire should extend so widely and last so long."[24] The exercise requires "us to go on to examine for what moral qualities and for what reason the true God deigned to help the Romans in the extension of their empire; for in his control are all the kingdoms of the earth."[25] It would be too hasty to conclude that Augustine is *justifying* the Roman Empire or providing an account of how God "blessed" it. To the contrary, Augustine's critique of Rome is trenchant: Rome, in his estimation, could only ever be unjust.[26] The question isn't about justifying the current regime; it is about discerning a way forward: When are we, what are we inheriting, what must we undo, what can we hope for, *given this history*?

If Augustine undertook such an exercise from a place of some privilege, such an exercise is not always and only an act of privilege. Discernment is not a baptism of the status quo. To read the Spirit's swerves in human history is not a matter of trying to sanctify when we are as "what God wants." Discernment is naming when we are, unveiling the systems and structures and histories that got us here, and then divining the avenues forward that give hope. In this regard, perhaps the most important "discernment work" always happens from the underside of history.

I'm reminded of a remarkable essay by Jesse McCarthy that explores the role for Black intellectuals today. When white supremacists "in ill-fitting khaki pants and tiki torches" were chanting the Nazi slogan "Blood and soil!" in a Charlottesville park, McCarthy thought back to David Walker's alternative formulation of "blood and tears." These, he notes, are two very different ways of imagining our bond to place. "An argument about whose blood is in the soil of this country is not an argument a white supremacist is going to win." But Walker, McCarthy notes, is working from a bolder conviction about the historical role that Black people in the United States have to play in the unfolding of world history. "He views, as I do, black Americans as a people bearing a unique historic destiny, a role to play in the history of the world that has everything to do with how we shape the country we find ourselves in."[27] The possibility is bound up with the tragedy, which doesn't for a second justify it or provide some retrospective way of redeeming slavery. Rather, it simply means that there is a different future possible that is embedded in this specific history. When, elsewhere, McCarthy hears the cry of protest and critique in the hip-hop genre of trap, again he locates this in time: "The force of our vernacular culture formed under slavery is the connection born principally in music, but also in the Word, in all of its manifold uses, that *believes in its own power*." Black culture isn't a natural kind or a metaphysical essence; it is the creation of a very particular history. The gift here, he hazards, is born of that history:

> Black culture isn't "magic" because of some deistic proximity of black people to the universe. Slavers had their cargo dance on deck to keep them limber for the auction block. The magic was born out of *a unique historical and material experience* in world history, one that no other group of people underwent and survived for so long and in such intimate proximity to the main engines of modernity.[28]

This is a risky reading of history. Some will all too eagerly glom onto this as a retrospective justification. But that's not what McCarthy is saying at all. Discernment is not a PR spin program for history. It is a prophetic endeavor that divines the future from the history we've been thrown into.

• • •

What it means to live faithfully and justly into a future is a question we can answer only if we take measure of the history that informs our present. Given a contingent, particular history—*facing* up to that history—the question is, What *now*? What's possible? To guide a faithful future, we need to know the past. This is the sort of orientation that a temporal compass offers.

Augustine offers a tool kit to help us calibrate our temporal compasses. This is not because we share the same history. In *City of God*, Augustine undertook the necessary work of discernment for a particular time and a particular place, and many of the particulars have little bearing on us in the twenty-first century. But our *task* is the same as his, and thus we have something to learn from *how* Augustine undertook this labor of temporal orientation. Moreover, Augustine models Gutiérrez's insight that human history is the temple of God.

In particular, Augustine bequeaths to us a couple of concepts that help us get our bearings. The first is his notion of the *saeculum*. Unlike our use of the word "secular," which we tend to associate with space (as in the "secular public square"), for Augustine the *saeculum* is an *era*, a chunk of history. The divine irruption in history that is the incarnation, cross, resurrection, and ascension—the Christ-event—becomes the Greenwich Mean of all history. In its shadow is the time in which we find ourselves: the era Augustine calls the *saeculum*, this age between cross and kingdom come. In other words, this long history in which we find ourselves—Auden's "Time Being"—is happening between the parentheses of God's incarnation in history and the full arrival of the kingdom in the parousia. It is the long spiritual escrow in which the poor are waiting to inherit the kingdom Jesus promised.

To simply remember that we inhabit the *saeculum* has significant implications for what to expect. For example, it means we should *expect pluralism*. While God's Spirit has been unleashed in history and in the church, the kingdom is not here yet. We shouldn't be shocked or scandalized by deep disagreement in the commonweal, so to speak.

The notion of the *saeculum* is related to the second idea I want to highlight from Augustine. His *City of God* is really a tale of two cities, which he describes as the "earthly" city and the "heavenly" city, or the city of man and the city of God. What distinguishes these two cities is not a realm or jurisdiction or levels, as if the earthly city was material and the heavenly city was ethereal. For Augustine, these two "cities" (Latin *civitas*, "republics") are distinguished by their loves, and the origin of the two cities is not creation but the Fall. In other words, the earthly city did not begin with time; it began *in* time, and more specifically as a result of the Fall. The two cities are two fundamentally different ways of being a human community that are organized around two very different sorts of love. The earthly city revolves around love of self and the lust for power and domination (the *libido dominandi*, Augustine calls it). The city of God revolves around love of God and engenders sacrifice for the neighbor.

Why does this matter for understanding time and history? Because in this era of the *saeculum*, Augustine emphasizes, we live in what he calls the *permixtum* of two cities. We will all find ourselves thrown into shared territories that are occupied by citizens of the earthly and heavenly cities who still need to figure out how to live together. The era of the *saeculum* is the long season in which we find ourselves "mixed up" with neighbors who share very different visions of the good. Ours is the time of wheat and tares, sheep and goats, deep differences lived out in close proximity.

Given that we inhabit the *saeculum*, what difference does this make for *how* we live in this era? What does it mean to be faithful in the *permixtum*?

Contra the utopianisms of both left and right, Christians are an *eschatological* people. That's what it means to not "live ahead of time," as Augustine puts it. If we remember that we live in the *saeculum*, in this contested time of waiting for the full realization of Christ's reign, we should not fall into the trap of thinking the kingdom has come. We shouldn't absolutize some penultimate regime or form of life. Those who thought the fall of Rome meant the collapse of the kingdom of God failed to see the distinction Augustine was making. Instead, they collapsed eschatological hope by settling for some present reality. When we do that, we forget how to wait. Eschatological expectation is essential to heavenly citizenship: as long as we're praying "Thy kingdom come," it's not here yet. That should undermine any temptation to identify a particular regime or government or party or policy or side or movement with the *arrival* of the kingdom—even if discernment also requires us to try to be attuned to movements that do bear the Spirit for a time and place.

This eschatological posture is characterized by a kind of holy impatience. On the one hand, we pray and labor for a world that looks more like the just, flourishing kingdom we long for. The "waiting" of Christian eschatology is not the same as what Dr. Martin Luther King Jr., in his "I Have a Dream" speech, called "the tranquilizing drug of gradualism," which used waiting as a code for enshrining the status quo.[29] On the other hand, even our properly prophetic desire and hunger must avoid becoming the hubris of human amelioration projects, as if we could socially engineer our way out of the brokenness of the world by our own ingenuity.

The British theologian Oliver O'Donovan puts it this way: the consequence of the Christ-event is a "'desacralization' of politics by the Gospel."[30] Politics and the shared work of forging a common life is a creaturely calling built into creation itself. But our earthly, political endeavors, even our most sincere endeavors on behalf of justice, can't *make* the kingdom come. Politics isn't everything precisely because we worship an ascended King. So Christians above all should not fall prey to the temptation to treat our meantime political identities as ultimate identities.

We are most prone to absolutize the temporal when our ultimate conviction is that there is no eternity, no kingdom coming. Hence a secularized society is apt to treat politics as everything, and hence treat political differences as if they were ultimate differences (my political opponent doesn't just disagree; he is *evil*). This betrays a stunted imagination that should not characterize Christians: while we are not indifferent, we know that justice will ultimately only arrive with the King. Even though it is precisely the vision of God's coming kingdom that motivates us to work for justice, recognizing our temporal location in the *saeculum* should temper our expectations and our relationship with those who disagree. This should also engender a Christian realism and the lost art of "faithful compromise."[31]

• • •

When we "read" history, looking for the contrails of the Spirit, the seeds of possibility left by God's providence and the snowballing effects of the people of God in history, we are trying to recognize the legacies of God's action in history. We are trying to discern the ways that our institutions and practices and habits bear the mark of God's grace. This, O'Donovan says, is a particular kind of archaeology: "Like the surface of a planet pocked with craters by the bombardment it receives from space, the governments of the passing age show the impact of Christ's dawning glory."[32] God's gifts are not just miraculous incursions into the present, they are more often legacies of God's influence on the cosmos handed down to us in the snowball effects of history.

For example, there are many ways in which the institutions and practices of liberal democracy are the distinct fruit of Christianity's impact on the political institutions of the West and (now) wider world. The political goods of representation, checks on power, even mercy in judgment, are distinct effects of the encounter between the gospel and political life.[33] And the legacy of that redemptive impact of grace on our common life is a gift that benefits many of those of other faiths and those with no faith at all. It is a legacy that shines upon the just and the unjust, so to speak.

However, this legacy is often erased from our collective memory in late modernity. One of the tasks of Christian public theology is a kind of *amnesia therapy* for our neighbors who prize the goods and institutions of democracy but somehow imagine they sit in tension with Christianity. (This will include a growing number of Christians who seem to think Christian commitment is antithetical to constitutional democracy and seem attracted to strongmen.) Christian political theology has a public role to play simply by renarrating to late-modern liberal societies their religious and theological inheritance.

• • •

Like the time our phones were unwittingly picking up a signal from a different time zone, it is easy for our spiritual timekeeping to become synced with something other than God's kingdom time. We might default to the *Zeitgeist*, for instance, or synchronize our watches with some alleged golden age, effectively freezing God's activity in some epoch when we should be making friends with the future. In many ways, our assimilation to cultural defaults is temporal. We start keeping time according to a different mean.

Our tendency to sync to something other than God's kingdom time makes ongoing liturgical recalibration necessary. This is especially true, I believe, if we are going to be animated by a properly eschatological orientation to the future. Hope takes practice.

Consider, for example, a crucial moment in the church's liturgical calendar that rehearses this reality as a reminder, year after year. At the very end of the liturgical year we observe the feast of Christ our King, and the very next Sunday is the beginning of Advent. In the feast of Christ the King we are reminded that the crucified God ascended to a throne while bearing his scars. If Christ is King, then all earthly rulers have, in a sense, already been deposed—they are merely stewards in the meantime. They can make no ultimate claims on us. When King Jesus knows the number of hairs on your head, you can't be reduced to a cog in some collectivist machine. Oliver O'Donovan calls this "the 'desacralization' of politics by the Gospel."

But Advent is how we learn to *wait*: not in passive quietism, not in Pelagian activism, but in hopeful trust. The kingdom is something we await, not create. The practice of Advent patience pushes back on the Christian temptation to "live ahead of time." Advent patience refuses right-wing theonomies that would forget this waiting and try to install the kingdom by political machinations. But it equally pushes back on any progressive utopianism that imagines that the full arrival of justice could be achieved by our efforts at social amelioration. Both of these are practical postmillennialisms that assume that the arrival of the kingdom is up to us—and hence something we should fight to impose. Both of these are failures to live into the realities of Christ the King and the waiting of Advent—not to mention the cross-shaped life of a people who image Christ. The rhythms of the church's life together offer an opportunity to practice our way into this eschatological imagination in a way that shapes how we are *sent*.

Heavenly citizens know what time it is. We are awaiting a coming King. Our expectations are disciplined by this eschatology. But that does not excuse us from the creaturely calling to respond to creation's own call for political realization, the call to build institutions and practices and habitualities that are foretastes of forthcoming *shalom*. In other words, the cultural work of creating polities is demanded by the very nature of creation, ever since creation, and still in this *saeculum* in which we find ourselves. The cross, resurrection, and new creation do not displace that calling; they renew it. In particular, the Christ-event reframes that calling as a call to love our neighbors, to create polities and policies, systems and institutions that protect the vulnerable, caring for the widows, orphans, and strangers among us while also making room for us to pursue an array of creaturely callings in commerce, education, the arts, and even our play. So we participate and collaborate in the *permixtum*, the contested but good space of our life in common, and we do so in ways that hope to bend, if ever so slightly, the earthly city toward the city of God.

Christian political participation should be bold but circumspect, tempered but hopeful, cross-shaped but kingdom bent. An eschatological life is one animated by the cadences of two hopeful exhortations: "Lift up your hearts" and "Be not afraid."

• • •

The name for this elongation of the soul toward the future, this holy impatience, this sacred hunger, is hope. Hope is a disposition toward the future that is at once expectant and dependent. It is entwined with faith because it trusts that the God of grace is a father who gives bread rather than stone (Matt. 7:9–11). And hope is bound to love because it is a form of desire. Thus Abraham, the father of faith, is also the paradigm of hope: "For he was looking forward to the city with foundations, whose architect and builder is God" (Heb. 11:10 NIV). He acts, obeys, goes, and yet there is an ultimate sense in which the city is built by the Creator. The city of God is a gift that descends (Rev. 21:2), even if that city also takes up our faithful labors as anticipations of its coming (Isa. 60). Gutiérrez gets at this braided relation of faith, hope, and love by way of the French poet and writer Charles Péguy: "Péguy has written that hope, which seemed to be led by her two older sisters, faith and charity, actually leads them. But this will be true only if hope in the future seeks roots in the present, if it takes shape in daily events with their joys to experience but also with their injustices to eliminate and their enslavements from which to be liberated."[34]

William Gibson, the father of cyberpunk, once quipped: "The future is already here, it's just not very evenly distributed."[35] This is an eschatological intuition: with the resurrection, the future of the cosmos has already arrived. But that future is not evenly distributed, which is why hope also finds its expression in lament. Christian hope refuses both Pollyannaish optimism and despairing nihilism.[36] "Optimists," Terry Eagleton points out, "are as bereft of hope as nihilists because they have no need of it."[37] The sense of *need* is what distinguishes hope from self-confidence or the hubris of mere progress.

The hymnbook of hope is organized around two repeated refrains: "How long, O Lord?" and *Maranatha!* "How long, O Lord?" is the protest-question posed to God precisely because we've witnessed the inbreaking of the kingdom. So why, Lord, delay its distribution? The persistence of hunger and violence, racism and exclusion, greed and plutocracy, addiction and abandonment are all affronts to the restored creation we've already seen in the resurrected Jesus. "How long, O Lord?" is the question of a hopeful people precisely because we are expecting the world promised in the Christ-event. The church is rightly impatient in this long pilgrimage. "How long, O Lord?" is the "Are we there yet?" of an eager people.

*Maranatha!* ("Come, Lord!") is a cry that is half plea and half imperative. Sometimes it is a cry for rescue: Come, Lord, and bring an end to these enduring injustices. Come, Lord, and save us from the henchman of Mammon grinding the poor underfoot. Come, Lord, and rescue those drowning in the sea. At other times, *Maranatha!* is a hungry cry for more of the good we already enjoy: Come, Lord, and make this fleeting joy permanent and stable. Come, Lord, and bind us together forever as we've experienced it in this moment. Come, Lord, and let your reconciliation ripple across the cosmos as we've just experienced in our community. More, please! Always! Forever!

The trick, the feat, the graced posture we are called to cultivate *on the way* is faithful labor in the present, rooted in discernment, always with our eyes on that coming city. I can still recall the lesson from my driver's ed class decades ago: "Aim high," the teacher told us. When you're driving, don't look immediately in front of you. If you're fixated on the immediate, your driving will always be reactive, and reactive drivers are dangerous drivers. While it might seem that they are perpetually on guard, in fact they are less able to absorb what's coming. Instead, aim high: look down the road and trust your peripheral vision. Let the way forward be guided by that longer view and you'll actually be a better driver. This long view, aiming high, is the posture of expectant humility so well described by Reinhold Niebuhr:

> Nothing that is worth doing can be achieved in our lifetime; therefore we must be saved by hope. Nothing which is true or beautiful or good makes complete sense in any immediate context of history; therefore we must be saved by faith. Nothing we do, however virtuous, can be accomplished alone; therefore we are saved by love. No virtuous act is quite as virtuous from the standpoint of our friend or foe as it is from our standpoint.

> Therefore we must be saved by the final form of love which is forgiveness.[38]

• • •

While an eschatological orientation will be characterized by a kind of holy impatience, there should also be something unhurried about an eschatological people. Our frenetic busyness is so often a practical outworking of an unconscious despair, for it is a refusal of hope. It is a refusal of hope because it is, functionally, a refusal of trust and dependence. When I am frantically busy, I subtly (or not so subtly) am assuming that everything depends on me, as if I'm the one upholding the cosmos, as if the arrival of the kingdom depends on me. There is an urgency that comes from a desire to see God's reign realized; but there is another kind of urgency we manufacture to make ourselves feel needed. "They ain't all waitin' on you," Ellis tells the sheriff in *No Country for Old Men*. "That's vanity."

I found myself profoundly convicted while reading Winn Collier's moving portrait of Eugene Peterson in his biography, *A Burning in My Bones*. Collier recalls a pivotal moment in Peterson's life, on the edge of burnout and despair, when he realized he was living as if everything depended on him—as if they were all waitin' on him. He expressed the longing to be "unhurried," and once unbottled, the words spilled out as he admitted to the church council:

> I want to be a pastor who prays. I want to be reflective and responsive and relaxed in the presence of God so that I can be reflective and responsive and relaxed in your presence. I can't do that on the run. It takes a lot of time. . . . It demands some detachment and perspective. I can't do this just by trying harder. I want to be a pastor who has the time to be with you in lei-

> surely, unhurried conversations so that I can understand and be a companion with you.[39]

The rest of the story is about the long, arduous work of becoming that sort of unhurried person. I experienced this like a smack in the face and yet also like a stained-glass portrait of a way of being I long for. To be unhurried is a tangible discipline of hope.

One of the scandals of an eschatological orientation is that it makes room for rest despite everything that needs to be done. Sabbath is its own expression of hope. While Sabbath obviously echoes creation, taking up the practice of Sabbath and the discipline of leisure expresses an eschatological orientation, a sense of trust and hope that God is always and ever acting in, around, beneath, and sometimes even in spite of our own labor. And so we can rest.

One of my teachers, Calvin Seerveld, talks about rest not just in terms of vacations and retreats and periodic stoppages of our drive for productivity, but rather a sort of leisure that is woven into our work, a *way* of living and working and being that has room for us to breathe. In his colorful prose, Seerveld observes that our "pragmatist culture and Agent no. 666 mentality squeeze leisure out of ordinary life." In contrast, he says,

> A biblical conception of leisure for me is that ample time becomes a coefficient of one's daily work activity. In the gospel story I read, the apostles, through the pressure of their kingdom work, did not have enough time to sit down for a meal; "Let's take a break," said Jesus. When you have enough time in what you are humanly doing, you have leisure. When there is time for you to move around in unpremeditatedly, you experience leisure. When it is possible for you to enter into an unexpected opportunity that arises, you are blessed with leisure.[40]

Leisure is an eschatological discipline of stilling hubris and resting in the God who has raised Jesus as the firstfruits of what is to come. "Having enough time" is an act of hope. Building margins into a life so you can respond to opportunities to muse, play, talk, pray is its own defiant act of trust and expectation.

• • •

We sing *Maranatha!* but we are not a panicked people. As the writer Marilynne Robinson once said, "Fear is not a Christian habit of mind."[41] That is not to condone apathy but rather to encourage hope, a way of laboring toward a future that arrives as a gift. This is rooted in a profound trust in a God who is a giver all the way down, a Creator whose creation is the first grace. To not panic is to live in the confidence that God's first and last word is love, no matter when we are.

# EPILOGUE

## *History in Heaven*

> Eternity is in love with the productions of time.
>
> —William Blake, *Proverbs of Hell*

One semester while I was teaching in Washington, DC, we visited Church of the Advent, where my friend Tommy Hinson is rector. That Sunday, the post-Communion prayer was one I had never encountered before, and in some ways, I think this book was conceived in the moment of that prayer. It goes like this:

> O God of our ancestors, God of our people, before whose face the human generations pass away: We thank you that in you we are kept safe forever, and that the broken fragments of our history are gathered up in the redeeming act of your dear Son, remembered in this holy sacrament of bread and wine. Help us to walk daily in the Communion of Saints, declaring our faith in the forgiveness of sins and the resurrection of the body. Now send us out in the power of your Holy Spirit to live and work for your praise and glory. Amen.

Tommy later told me the prayer comes from a liturgy developed by the Anglican Church of the Province of Kenya, forged in the late 1980s, as an expression of an ancient faith that also spoke to the needs and sorrows and hopes of East Africa.

It was this phrase that stopped me short, as the sort of prayer I had never encountered in other European streams: "The broken fragments of our history are gathered up in the redeeming act of your dear Son."

I do recall, early in my Christian pilgrimage, when a friend from Chicago pointed me to a passage in the minor prophet Joel that is perhaps familiar to many: "I will repay you for the years that the swarming locust has eaten," the Lord promises (Joel 2:25). I still remember this as one of my first encounters with a conviction that animates this book: that the Lord of the star fields and Creator of the cosmos was attuned to the specificity and particularity of the histories we have endured in time, addressing the strange and perplexing ways we carry absence and loss in our heart and bones, the way a profound *lack* could exert so much power on our lives. From my earliest reading in the Gospels, I had come to understand that God knew the number of hairs on my head. But somehow it was a moving revelation to realize that God also saw what I had lived through—that the eternal God understood what I had lost, what had been missing, what the locusts had eaten and left me bereft of. In Joel's prophetic word I heard a promise of restoration attuned to *my* history—the promise of an abundant God not only making up for the lack but wantonly overflowing the cup.

I should testify that this has indeed been the measure of God's grace to me. If I have walked through life with a limp because of the absence of a father, with only memories of apathy and terror in his place, God has restored what the locust has eaten by granting me the profound, daunting, miraculous opportunity to *be* a father. By God's grace, Deanna and I have spent over thirty years invested in the time-bending maneuver called a family, trying to turn back the curse of generations. Graced with friends who surround us and mentors as models, God called us to something new which is this family, with four remarkable, forgiving children in whom the cup of joy and love overflows for us. My past was restored in a future I could never have imagined, embodied in the children who made me a father: Grayson, Coleson, Madison, and Jackson. It's not that the locust didn't rob me of something; but we eat in plenty now (Joel 2:26).

But there's still something unique going on in this prayer from Kenya. This "gathering up" of *our* history is a beautiful expression of spiritual timekeeping that is too often absent from individualist nowhen Christianities of the West in the age of late capitalism. Redemption, here, does not sweep away a past; rather, Christ's redemption gathers up the broken fragments and *makes* something of them. The God who saves is a mosaic artist who takes the broken fragments of our history and does a new thing: he creates a work of art in which that history is reframed, reconfigured, taken up, and reworked such that the mosaic could only be what it is *with* that history. The consummation of time is not the erasure of history. The end of all things is a "taking up," not a destruction. "Time was not made for death but for eternity."[1]

• • •

If God's redemption gathers up the broken fragments of our histories into a mosaic of new life, it seems like those histories go with us to heaven too. We will arrive in the kingdom of God carrying our stories. Indeed, if Christ's resurrection is the firstfruits, we will arrive at the marriage supper of the Lamb with our scars. It's hard not to imagine someone at that banquet of joy turning to ask, "Tell me about that scar," and somehow, in ways that are unthinkable to me now, I will be able to revisit my history without pain or trauma, not because the memory card of my mind has been erased but because now I can see only the unique mosaic that is redeemed, rescued *me*, the tapestry that is *us*.

Don't ask me for chapter and verse on this; I'm not very bothered by the dogmatic particulars. I'll simply invoke the beautiful longing articulated by my ancient friend, St. Augustine. In his *Confessions*, Augustine recalls one of his dearest and oldest friends, Nebridius, who has since died and now lives, as he puts it, "in Abraham's bosom" (Luke 16:22). The normally confident Augustine isn't quite sure just what that means, but whatever it symbolizes, he says, "that is where my Nebridius lives, a sweet friend to me, but, Lord, your former freedman and now adopted son." His sweet friend who used to pepper Augustine with all sorts of questions about God, with whom he enjoyed years of boisterous back-and-forth, the sorts of tête-à-têtes that feel like pure joy. But his friend is now gone. He is no longer asking questions; instead, Augustine imagines how he "avidly drinks as much as he can of wisdom, happy without end." And yet, Augustine muses, "I do not think him so intoxicated by that as to forget me, since you, Lord, whom he drinks, are mindful of us."[2]

There is Nebridius in heaven, enjoying the bliss of the beatific vision, and Augustine can't help but imagine that Nebridius carries their shared history with him into the presence of God. He bears the imprint of his friendships in the kingdom. Nebridius will never not be someone who was Augustine's friend.

Redemption is not an undoing, an effacing, or an erasing but a "gathering up" of our histories, a taking up of what time has wrought. Like the ships of Tarshish (Isa. 60:9), our habitualities and history sail into an eternal future with a God who makes all things new. Eternity bears the marks of our now.

# ACKNOWLEDGMENTS

I don't think I've taken the full measure of how much an encounter with Gustavo Gutiérrez's *Theology of Liberation* in the mid-1990s has shaped my thinking over the years. That influence has been subterranean, and working on this book brought it back to the surface. In many ways, this book is just an extended homage to Gutiérrez's chapter 10, "Encountering God in History," and his signal claim: "God's temple is human history."

A first glimmer of an idea that became this book germinated because of a talk I was invited to give in the House of Lords in November 2018. My thanks to the Christians in Parliament organization for the invitation and generative conversation.

My friends Rev. Kenny Benge and Rev. Eric Dirksen read a draft of this book and offered both helpful feedback and timely encouragement. I'm grateful for their kindness.

I don't know if it's possible to thank a place, but this book owes many debts to Laity Lodge. The Lodge is a geography of tranquility for me, its rivers and cliffs and vistas a balm for my soul. But my deepest thanks go to the dear friends there who have welcomed us and made it feel like a spiritual home away from home for us (including in some harrowing times!). This was especially true during a residency in fall 2021 in which I finished the final version of this book. One of my goals was for this book to *feel* like the Lodge, and I hope some of its spirit has seeped in. Our sincerest thanks to the whole team—Gate, Grant, Tim, Ryan, and others—for such life-giving hospitality. But a special thanks to our friends Amy and Steven Purcell for your kindness and warmth. I want to be Steven Purcell when I grow up.

I continue to be thankful for the team at Brazos, who warmly welcome my work, provide encouragement along the way, and collaborate with me on every facet of turning inchoate ideas into the beautiful books they produce. I don't ever want to take for granted how much you let me be part of the process. So thank you to Kara and Paula and Shelly and the rest of the team for your openness and support, and to Eric Salo for his help improving my prose. A special thanks to Bob Hosack and Jeremy Wells for being my champions.

As ever, always, forever, my deepest gratitude goes to Deanna: partner, friend, co-pilgrim. You met me when I was a boy; the man I've become bears all the fingerprints of your grace and love. We spend a lot of time together, and it's still never enough. Your help and encouragement at the eleventh hour of this project made all the difference.

Per my usual custom, you'll find a *How to Inhabit Time* playlist on Spotify that includes songs mentioned in the book, as well as others that were on rotation while I wrote this. For me, this book will always sound like a mix of Phoebe Bridgers, Erik Satie, and Sufjan Stevens's marvelous meditations in *Convocations*.

# NOTES

## Preface

1. Charles Taylor, *Hegel* (Cambridge: Cambridge University Press, 1975), 73.

2. Rainer Maria Rilke, "Archaic Torso of Apollo," Poets.org, https://poets.org/poem/archaic-torso-apollo.

## Introduction

1. David Farrier, "We're Gonna Carry That Weight a Long Time," *Emergence Magazine*, May 12, 2021, https://emergencemagazine.org/essay/were-gonna-carry-that-weight-a-long-time.

2. I am adopting this term "nowhen" from Jimena Canales, *The Physicist and the Philosopher: Einstein, Bergson, and the Debate That Changed Our Understanding of Time* (Princeton: Princeton University Press, 2015), 103.

3. And what we imagine as a possible future for such questions and challenges is also a factor of the history that got us here. On the question of race and racism, I would especially commend Jonathan Tran's bold argument in *Asian Americans and the Spirit of Racial Capitalism* (New York: Oxford University Press, 2021). To live in the modernity of capitalism, Tran argues, is to be an inevitable heir of race and anti-racism. But that doesn't settle what the future of racial identity looks like, and—as Tran argues—too much anti-racism treats the historical emergence of race as natural rather than cultural.

4. Augustine, *Confessions* 11.25.32, trans. Henry Chadwick (Oxford: Oxford University Press, 1992), 239.

5. James Baldwin, "The White Man's Guilt," *Ebony* 20, no. 10 (August 1965): 47–48, reprinted in *James Baldwin: Collected Essays* (New York: Library of America, 1998), 722–23.

6. James Baldwin interview, "How Can We Get the Black People to Cool It?," *Esquire*, July 1, 1978, cited in Eddie S. Glaude Jr., *Begin Again: James Baldwin's America and Its Urgent Lessons for Our Own* (New York: Crown, 2020), 68.

7. Judith Sutera, *St. Benedict's Rule: An Inclusive Translation and Daily Commentary* (Collegeville, MN: Liturgical Press, 2021), 51.

8. Søren Kierkegaard, *Philosophical Fragments / Johannes Climacus*, ed. and trans. Howard V. Hong and Edna H. Hong (Princeton: Princeton University Press, 1985), 13.

9. Kierkegaard, *Philosophical Fragments*, 18.

10. O. K. Bouwsma, "Faith, Evidence, and Proof," in *Without Proof or Evidence: Essays of O. K. Bouwsma*, ed. J. L. Craft and Ronald E. Hustwit (Lincoln: University of Nebraska Press, 1984), 6.

11. Bouwsma, "Faith, Evidence, and Proof," 7.

12. Martin Heidegger, "Phenomenology and Theology," trans. James G. Hart and John C. Maraldo, in *Pathmarks*, ed. William McNeill (Cambridge: Cambridge University Press, 1998).

13. Heidegger, "Phenomenology and Theology," 44–46.

14. Augustine, *Confessions* 11.25.32 (trans. Chadwick, 239).

15. Annie Dillard, *For the Time Being* (New York: Vintage, 2000), 88.

16. The term comes from 1 Samuel 4 where, after the capture of the ark of the covenant by the Philistines, the wife of Phinehas gives birth to a son and, while dying, names him "Ichabod" ("no glory") because "the glory has departed from Israel" (1 Sam. 4:22).

17. Lionel Salter, *Going to a Concert* (London: Penguin, 1954), 16–17.

## Chapter 1: Creatures of Time

1. Jeremy Cooper, *Ash before Oak* (London: Fitzcarraldo Editions, 2019), 175.

2. Augustine, *Confessions* 11.31.41, trans. Henry Chadwick (Oxford: Oxford University Press, 1992), 245.

3. Tim O'Brien, *The Things They Carried* (Boston: Mariner, 2009), 7.

4. It is perhaps worth noting that, like myself, Dallas Willard, a leading voice in helping us understand spiritual formation, was a specialist in phenomenology. For relevant discussion, see Gary W. Moon, *Becoming Dallas Willard: The Formation of a Philosopher, Teacher, and Christ Follower* (Downers Grove, IL: InterVarsity, 2018), 223–24.

5. For a helpful elucidation of these ideas in Husserl, see Anthony J. Steinbock, *Home and Beyond: Generative Phenomenology after Husserl* (Evanston, IL: Northwestern University Press, 1995), 29–33.

6. For discussion of these themes, see Edmund Husserl, *Cartesian Meditations: An Introduction to Phenomenology*, trans. Dorion Cairns (The Hague: Martinus Nijhoff, 1960), 66–68.

7. "For example," Husserl says, "if, in an act of judgment, I decide for the first time in favor of a being and a being-thus, the fleeting act passes; but from now on *I am abidingly the Ego who is thus and so decided*." Edmund Husserl, *Cartesian Meditations: An Introduction to Phenomenology*, trans. Dorion Cairns (Dordrecht: Kluwer Academic, 1993), 66.

8. See Helen Ngo, "Racist Habits: A Phenomenological Analysis of Racism and the Habitual Body," *Philosophy and Social Criticism* 42, no. 9 (November 2016): 847–72.

9. Steinbock, *Home and Beyond*, 223.

10. It is downplayed and ignored often because of implicit but misguided theological assumptions that if we believe in a sovereign God and providential care, then nothing could be contingent. But, in fact, it is precisely a theology of creation ex nihilo that makes contingency fundamental to creation.

11. T. S. Eliot, "Burnt Norton," the first of his *Four Quartets* (Boston: Mariner, 1971), 13–21. Compare the oft-overlooked ballad by Little Texas, "What Might Have Been."

12. Martin Heidegger, *Being and Time*, trans. Joan Stambaugh (Albany, NY: SUNY Press, 1996), 127, 167.

13. Heidegger was likely influenced by Kierkegaard in this respect. Consider, for example, this passage in *Repetition* that has something of the Talking Heads about it, with flashes of Job: "Where am I? What does it mean to say: the world? What is the meaning of that word? Who tricked me into this whole thing and leaves me standing here? Who am I? How did I get into the world? Why was I not asked about it, why was I not informed of the rules and regulations but just thrust into the ranks as if I had been bought from a peddling shanghaier of human beings? How did I get involved in this big enterprise called actuality? Why should I be involved? Isn't it a matter of choice? And if I am compelled to be involved, where is the manager—I have something to say about this. Is there no manager? To whom shall I make my complaint?" Søren Kierkegaard, *Fear and Trembling / Repetition*, ed. and trans. Howard V. Hong and Edna H. Hong (Princeton: Princeton University Press, 1983), 200. Cf. Ivan Karamazov on his "ticket." Fyodor Dostoevsky, *The Brothers Karamazov*, trans. Richard Pevear and Larissa Volokhonsky (New York: Farrar, Straus & Giroux, 2002), 245.

14. I allude, gently, to Stephen Greenblatt, *The Swerve: How the World Became Modern* (New York: Norton, 2011).

15. William Faulkner, *Requiem for a Nun* (New York: Vintage, 1994), 73.

16. Katie Holten, "Stone Alphabet," *Emergence Magazine* 2 (2021): 20–21, available at https://emergencemagazine.org/gallery/stone-alphabet.

17. See recent books by Yuval Levin such as *The Fractured Republic: Renewing America's Social Contract in the Age of Individualism* (New York: Basic Books, 2016) and *A Time to Build: From Family and Community to*

*Congress and the Campus, How Recommitting to Our Institutions Can Revive the American Dream* (New York: Basic Books, 2020).

18. Avett Brothers, "We Americans," on *Closer Than Together*, Republic/Universal, 2019. Used by permission.

19. Apsley Cherry-Garrard, *The Worst Journey in the World: Antarctic, 1910–1913* (Guilford, CT: Lyons, 2004), 232.

20. In this way, another anesthetizing form of relating to the past is a different instantiation of nostalgia. "Primitivism" posits that all that is good and true and beautiful can only be found "at the origin," whether that's the first century of the church or the founding of the American republic. The long history between that origin and our present is narrated as a downfall and departure, a long era of absence—of the Spirit or Truth or what have you—which only a later revival can recover. There might be a sense in which primitivism is the default posture of American evangelicalism, which finds its legacy in revivalism. This stands in direct opposition to catholicity.

21. Quoted in Tyler Estep, "Roy Faulkner, the Man Who Carved Stone Mountain, Dead at 84," *Atlanta Journal-Constitution*, September 23, 2016, https://www.ajc.com/news/local/roy-faulkner-the-man-who-carved-stone-mountain-dead/Eq2sjhjPM1EwDpDYLi4W0L.

22. A. E. Stallings, "Summer of the Statue Storm," *Image* 106 (2020): 103–4.

23. Stallings, "Summer of the Statue Storm."

24. See Richard H. Thaler and Cass R. Sunstein, *Nudge: Improving Decisions about Health, Wealth, and Happiness* (New York: Penguin, 2009), 139.

25. Thomas Aquinas, *Summa Theologiae*, II-II, Q. 20, trans. Fathers of the English Dominican Province (New York: Benziger Bros., 1947), available at https://aquinas101.thomisticinstitute.org/st-index.

26. Matthew Aucoin, "A Dance to the Music of Death," *New York Review of Books*, May 13, 2021, 8, available at https://www.nybooks.com/articles/2021/05/13/thomas-ades-dance-to-the-music-of-death.

27. Note, for example, J. N. Findlay's claim in his foreword to an English edition of Hegel's *Phenomenology of Spirit*: "The Christian God is essentially redemptive, and Hegel's philosophy is essentially a philosophy of redemption, of a self-alienation that returns to self in victory. If Hegel was nothing better, he was at least a great Christian theologian." Findlay, foreword to *Phenomenology of Spirit*, by G. W. F. Hegel, trans. A. V. Miller (Oxford: Oxford University Press, 1977), xxvii. For an analysis that both confirms and complicates this claim, see Cyril O'Regan, *The Heterodox Hegel* (Albany, NY: SUNY Press, 1994).

28. Charles Taylor, *Hegel* (Cambridge: Cambridge University Press, 1975), 68–69.

29. This is at the conclusion of the preface to Hegel's *Elements of the Philosophy of Right*, trans. H. B. Nisbet, ed. Allen W. Wood (Cambridge: Cambridge University Press, 1991), 23.

30. Marilynne Robinson, *Gilead* (New York: Farrar, Straus & Giroux, 2004), 91.
31. Hegel, *Elements of the Philosophy of Right*, 23.
32. Taylor, *Hegel*, 73.
33. Taylor, *Hegel*, 73.
34. Reinhold Niebuhr, *The Irony of American History* (1952), in *Reinhold Niebuhr: Major Works in Religion and Politics*, ed. Elisabeth Sifton (New York: Library of America, 2015), 523.
35. Niebuhr, *Irony of American History*, 576.
36. Niebuhr, *Irony of American History*, 510.
37. Niebuhr, *Irony of American History*, 576.
38. Niebuhr, *Irony of American History*, 585.
39. Niebuhr, *Irony of American History*, 586. Niebuhr's remark, in 1952, was aimed at the pretensions of Communism, but the analysis seems applicable more widely today.
40. Niebuhr, *Irony of American History*, 585.
41. Niebuhr, *Irony of American History*, 585.
42. Niebuhr, *Irony of American History*, 586.
43. Niebuhr, *Irony of American History*, 587.

## Chapter 2: A History of the Human Heart

1. Barry Lopez, *Arctic Dreams: Imagination and Desire in a Northern Landscape* (1986; repr., New York: Vintage, 2001), 20.
2. Lopez, *Arctic Dreams*, 29.
3. Lopez, *Arctic Dreams*, 29.
4. Peter Wayne Moe, *Touching This Leviathan* (Corvallis: Oregon State University Press, 2021), 120.
5. Moe, *Touching This Leviathan*, 121.
6. Moe, *Touching This Leviathan*, 48.
7. Moe, *Touching This Leviathan*, 106, quoting Kathleen Jamie, *Sightlines* (London: Sort of Books, 2012), 97.
8. See Thomas Wolfe, *You Can't Go Home Again* (New York: Scribner, 1934).
9. Heidegger, *Being and Time*, trans. John Macquarrie and Edward Robinson (New York: Harper & Row, 1962), 183. Heidegger uses a technical term to describe human beings, not as "subjects" but as *Dasein*, which means, quite literally translated, "being-there." Humans are distinctly defined by their locatedness, as finite creatures who always live at the intersection of time and place. In that spirit, perhaps we could also describe *Dasein* as *Dannsein*, "being-*then*," to indicate our locatedness in time.
10. Martin Heidegger, *Being and Time*, trans. Joan Stambaugh (Albany, NY: SUNY Press, 1996), 135.
11. Heidegger, *Being and Time*, 135 (trans. Stambaugh, slightly modified). I have transposed Heidegger's technical term *Dasein* into the first-person "I."

12. Wendell Berry, "Manifesto: The Mad Farmer Liberation Front," in *The Selected Poems of Wendell Berry* (Berkeley: Counterpoint, 1998), 87–88.

13. I am considering some of the unique temporal dynamics of shame. For a more robust discussion, see Brené Brown, *I Thought It Was Just Me (But It Isn't)* (New York: Avery, 2007), particularly on "shame-resilience."

14. See 2 Cor. 12:1–10 and Leonard Cohen's song, "Anthem," lyrics in *Leonard Cohen: Poems and Songs*, ed. Robert Faggen (New York: Knopf, 1993), 188.

15. Cf. Brené Brown, *The Gifts of Imperfection: Let Go of Who You Think You're Supposed to Be and Embrace Who You Are* (Center City, MN: Hazelden, 2010).

16. Nicholas Samaras, "Beloved Ghosts of Geography," *Image* 108 (2021): 91. Reprinted with permission. To hear the poet read this poem, visit https://imagejournal.org/article/beloved-ghosts-of-geography.

17. What I know about Sankofa I learned from an interview with the Appalachian novelist Crystal Wilkinson, "Go Back and Fetch It: A Conversation with Crystal Wilkinson," *Image* 108 (2021): 71, available at https://imagejournal.org/article/go-back-and-fetch-it-a-conversation-with-crystal-wilkinson.

18. Cf. the Christian camp version of "justification": "Just as if I'd never sinned."

19. It is perhaps worth noting that Paul the apostle, who heralds the new creation, can also appeal to his own prior formation as relevant to his ministry (2 Cor. 11:21–30).

20. Christine Smallwood, *The Life of the Mind* (New York: Hogarth, 2020), 104–5.

21. Karl Ove Knausgaard, *Winter*, trans. Ingvild Burkey (New York: Penguin, 2018), 128.

22. For philosophy geeks, this notion of God "taking up" our histories is a nod to Hegel's key verb, *aufheben*, which translators have struggled to render into English since the nineteenth century. The verb notes a complex movement of cancellation/preservation/elevation, "taking up" in the sense of both "taking away" and appropriating. This complex dynamic is exactly the strange power of God's redemptive action in history.

23. "Every Time I Hear That Song," words and music by Brandi Carlile, Phil Hanseroth, and Tim Hanseroth, Copyright © 2018 Universal Music Corp. and Southern Oracle Music, LLC, all rights administered by Universal Music Corp., all rights reserved, used by permission, reprinted by permission of Hal Leonard LLC.

24. Margaret Renkl, *Late Migrations: A Natural History of Love and Loss* (Minneapolis: Milkweed Editions, 2019), 217.

**Meditation 2**

1. Annie Dillard, *For the Time Being* (New York: Vintage, 2000), 88.

## Chapter 3: The Sacred Folds of *Kairos*

1. Olivier Clément, *Transfiguring Time: Understanding Time in the Light of the Orthodox Tradition*, trans. Jeremy N. Ingpen (Hyde Park, NY: New City, 2019), 39.

2. Michael Scholz-Hänsel, *El Greco: Domenikos Theotokopoulos* (Los Angeles: Taschen, 2011), 51.

3. Gaspar de Crayer, *Virgin with Child and Saints Maria Magdalen, Cecilia, Dorothea, Catherina, and Augustine*, 1638, Kunsthistorisches Museum Wien, Vienna, Austria, https://www.khm.at/objektdb/detail/555.

4. Clément, *Transfiguring Time*, 46, 48–49.

5. Søren Kierkegaard, *Philosophical Fragments / Johannes Climacus*, ed. and trans. Howard V. Hong and Edna H. Hong (Princeton: Princeton University Press, 1985), 61.

6. Cf. Markus Bockmuehl, "Introduction: Watching Luke Paint the Virgin" and "The Wisdom of the Implied Exegete," in *Seeing the Word: Refocusing New Testament Study* (Grand Rapids: Baker Academic, 2006), 13–25, 75–99.

7. Kierkegaard, *Philosophical Fragments*, 59.

8. Kierkegaard, *Philosophical Fragments*, 59–60.

9. Kierkegaard, *Philosophical Fragments*, 60.

10. Kierkegaard, *Philosophical Fragments*, 63.

11. Kierkegaard, *Philosophical Fragments*, 64–65.

12. Kierkegaard, *Philosophical Fragments*, 67.

13. Kierkegaard, *Philosophical Fragments*, 69.

14. Kierkegaard, *Philosophical Fragments*, 106.

15. Christine Smallwood, *The Life of the Mind* (New York: Hogarth, 2021), 13, 104.

16. Smallwood, *Life of the Mind*, 15.

17. Smallwood, *Life of the Mind*, 226.

18. Daniel Weidner, "Prophetic Criticism and the Rhetoric of Temporality: Paul Tillich's *Kairos* Texts and Weimar Intellectual Politics," *Political Theology* 21, nos. 1–2 (2020): 72.

19. Cf. Tomáš Halík, *I Want You to Be: On the God of Love*, trans. Gerald Turner (Notre Dame, IN: University of Notre Dame Press, 2016). My thanks to Steven Purcell for the gift of this book.

20. Søren Kierkegaard, *Repetition*, in *Fear and Trembling / Repetition*, ed. and trans. Howard V. Hong and Edna H. Hong (Princeton: Princeton University Press, 1983), 148–49. Earlier Kierkegaard tries to get at the paradoxical nature of what he's suggesting by contrasting "recollection" and "repetition": "Repetition and recollection are the same movement, except in opposite directions, for what is recollected has been, is repeated backward, whereas genuine repetition is recollected forward" (131).

21. Cf. Gustavo Gutiérrez on incarnation as the "fulfillment" of creation in *A Theology of Liberation: History, Politics, Salvation*, rev. ed., trans. Sister Caridad Inda and John Eagleson (Maryknoll, NY: Orbis, 1988), 86–109.

22. Robert Alter, *The Five Books of Moses: A Translation and Commentary* (New York: Norton, 2004), 872. My thanks to Vito Aiuto for pointing me to this insight.

23. Consider Charles Williams's marvelous dedication of *Descent of the Dove*, his book on church history: "To the Companions of the Co-inherence." Williams, *The Descent of the Dove: A Short History of the Holy Spirit in the Church* (New York: Longmans, Green, 1939).

24. Cited in Daniel Rosenberg, "Time," in *Curiosity and Method: Ten Years of Cabinet Magazine* (New York: Cabinet Books, 2012), 398–99. Rosenberg's essay is accompanied by a marvelous visualization, a timeline of timelines (400–405).

25. Rosenberg, "Time," 399.

26. Henri Bergson, *Matter and Memory*, trans. N. M. Paul and W. S. Palmer (New York: Zone Books, 1988), 207.

27. On Bergson's notion of time "melting" in duration, see Henri Bergson, *Creative Evolution* (Mineola, NY: Dover, 1998), 9–10. For an intriguing discussion of Bergson, see Thomas Martin's essay "On Time," included in the exhibit catalog for the Metropolitan Museum of Art's 2020 anniversary show, *About Time: Fashion and Duration*, ed. Andrew Boulton (New Haven: Yale University Press, 2020), xx–xxi.

28. My summary history in this paragraph is dependent on Allen W. Palmer, "Negotiation and Resistance in Global Networks: The 1884 International Meridian Conference," *Mass Communication and Society* 5, no. 1 (2002): 7–24.

29. Palmer, "Negotiation and Resistance in Global Networks," 13.

30. Lewis Mumford, *Technics and Civilization* (1934; repr., New York: Harcourt, Brace, 1963), 14.

31. Clair Wills, "Stepping Out," *New York Review of Books*, August 20, 2020, 4–5, available at https://www.nybooks.com/articles/2020/08/20/stepping-out. All quotations here and below come from this article.

## Chapter 4: Embrace the Ephemeral

1. Margaret Renkl, "Our Days Have Always Been Running Out," *New York Times*, September 20, 2020, https://www.nytimes.com/2020/09/20/opinion/our-days-have-always-been-running-out.html.

2. Charles Baudelaire, "The Painter of Modern Life," in *The Painter of Modern Life, and Other Essays*, trans. Jonathan Mayne (New York: Phaidon, 1964), 13. Baudelaire goes on to say that "the ephemeral, the fugitive, the contingent" is only half the story of modernism; the "other half," he says, "is the eternal and the immutable" (13).

3. This, in fact, is the argument of my first book, *The Fall of Interpretation: Philosophical Foundations for a Creational Hermeneutic* (Downers Grove, IL: InterVarsity, 2000).

4. Sally Mann, *Hold Still* (New York: Little, Brown, 2015), 300–302.

5. Listen to Jason Isbell's song "If We Were Vampires" on *The Nashville Sound*, Southeastern Records / Thirty Tigers, 2017.

6. Søren Kierkegaard, *Fear and Trembling / Repetition*, trans. Howard V. Hong and Edna H. Hong (Princeton: Princeton University Press, 1983), 41.

7. This is perhaps odd and not uncontroversial, but let's take a visceral example: the resurrected Jesus gets hungry and eats (Luke 24:43; John 21:12–15). Moreover, the hope of humanity is to be at the table for the marriage supper of the Lamb (Rev. 19:9). There is no digestion without change, and there is no change without time.

8. Augustine, *Confessions* 11.20.26, trans. Henry Chadwick (Oxford: Oxford Classics, 1992), 235.

9. Augustine, *Confessions* 11.28.38 (trans. Chadwick, 243).

10. Augustine, *Confessions* 11.31.41 (trans. Chadwick, 245). Admittedly, Augustine ultimately sees this distension as lamentable, a sign of our fallenness, and something from which we should hope to escape. I think he is more Platonic than Augustinian in that suggestion. For my critique of Augustine on this point, see James K. A. Smith, *The Fall of Interpretation: Philosophical Foundations for a Creational Hermeneutic*, 2nd ed. (Grand Rapids: Baker Academic, 2012), 154–56.

11. Cf. Jeremy Begbie's discussion of Olivier Messiaen's *Quartet for the End of Time* in *Resounding Truth: Christian Wisdom in the World of Music* (Grand Rapids: Baker Academic, 2007), 163–76. See also his seminal discussions in Begbie, *Theology, Music and Time*, Cambridge Studies in Christian Doctrine 4 (Cambridge: Cambridge University Press, 2000).

12. Peter J. Leithart, *Solomon among the Postmoderns* (Grand Rapids: Brazos, 2008), 66–68.

13. Robert Hudson, *The Poet and the Fly: Art, Nature, God, Mortality, and Other Elusive Mysteries* (Minneapolis: Broadleaf, 2020), 37. He cites Sam Hamill's introduction to Kobayashi Issa, *The Spring of My Life and Selected Haiku*, trans. Sam Hamill (Boston: Shambhala, 1997), xii.

14. Yoshida Kenkō, *Essays in Idleness: The Tsurezuregusa of Kenkō*, trans. and ed. Donald Keene (New York: Columbia University Press, 1967), 7.

15. The Nun Abutsu, "The First Order of Things: Feelings," trans. Hiroaki Sato, in *The Bliss of Reading: 40 Years of Poetry East*, ed. Richard Jones (Chicago: Poetry East, 2020), 128.

16. Elizabeth Bishop, "One Art," in *Poems* (New York: Farrar, Straus & Giroux, 2011), 198. Copyright © 2011 by The Alice H. Methfessel Trust. Publisher's Note and compilation copyright © 2011 by Farrar, Straus and Giroux. Reprinted by permission of Farrar, Straus and Giroux. All rights reserved.

17. Cf. George Bradley, "Penicillin and the Anthropocene Apocalypse," *Paris Review* 237 (Summer 2021), https://www.theparisreview.org/poetry/7811/penicillin-and-the-anthropocene-apocalypse-george-bradley.

18. Augustine, *Confessions* 4.9.14 (trans. Chadwick, 61), citing Tobit 13:18.

19. John Terpstra, *Skin Boat: Acts of Faith and Other Navigations* (Kentville, Nova Scotia: Gaspereau, 2009), 106.

20. Terpstra, *Skin Boat*, 19.

21. Augustine, *Of True Religion* 35.65, in *Augustine: Earlier Writings*, trans. and ed. John H. S. Burleigh (Philadelphia: Westminster, 1953), 258.

### Chapter 5: Seasons of the Heart

1. On a "view from nowhen," see Jimena Canales, *The Physicist and the Philosopher: Einstein, Bergson, and the Debate That Changed Our Understanding of Time* (Princeton: Princeton University Press, 2015), 102–3.

2. Alice Waters, *We Are What We Eat: A Slow Food Manifesto* (New York: Penguin, 2021), 124–25.

3. Waters, *We Are What We Eat*, 125.

4. Waters, *We Are What We Eat*, 125.

5. Waters, *We Are What We Eat*, 122.

6. Waters, *We Are What We Eat*, 120.

7. Waters, *We Are What We Eat*, 125.

8. A little *Matrix* allusion for those with ears to hear.

9. Pope Francis, *Gaudete et exsultate* §166, Vatican, March 19, 2018, https://www.vatican.va/content/francesco/en/apost_exhortations/documents/papa-francesco_esortazione-ap_20180319_gaudete-et-exsultate.html.

10. Pope Francis, *Gaudete et exsultate* §170.

11. Pope Francis, *Gaudete et exsultate* §169.

12. E. M. Forster, quoted in Spencer Reece, *All the Beauty Still Left: A Poet's Painted Book of Hours* (Brooklyn, NY: Turtle Point, 2021), n.p.

13. I should say: all discernment is ultimately communal discernment because even my "personal" life is intertwined with others. I am not an island.

14. Quite famously in this widely read article: Adam Grant, "There's a Name for the Blah You're Feeling: It's Called Languishing," *New York Times*, April 19, 2021, https://www.nytimes.com/2021/04/19/well/mind/covid-mental-health-languishing.html.

15. Apsley Cherry-Garrard, *The Worst Journey in the World: Antarctic, 1910–1913* (Guilford, CT: Lyons, 2004), 115–16.

16. That *this* murder rather than countless others should have finally been a catalyst is itself a mysterious constellation of historical moment.

17. We could talk about why such wisdom is better received from older friends than from parents.

18. See, e.g., Larry Diamond, "Democracy's Deepening Recession," *Atlantic*, May 2, 2014, https://www.theatlantic.com/international/archive/2014/05/the-deepening-recession-of-democracy/361591.

19. Pope Francis, remarks given at the opening of the Synod of Bishops on Young People, the Faith, and Vocational Discernment, Vatican, October 3, 2018, https://www.vatican.va/content/francesco/en/speeches/2018/october/documents/papa-francesco_20181003_apertura-sinodo.html.

20. John XXIII, address on the Solemn Opening of the Second Vatican Council, October 11, 1962, quoted in Pope Francis, remarks given at the

opening of the Synod of Bishops on Young People, the Faith, and Vocational Discernment, Vatican, October 3, 2018, https://www.vatican.va/content/francesco/en/speeches/2018/october/documents/papa-francesco_20181003_apertura-sinodo.html.

21. Michel Foucault, "Nietzsche, Genealogy, History," in *Language, Counter-Memory, Practice: Selected Essays and Interviews*, trans. Donald F. Bouchard and Sherry Simon (Ithaca, NY: Cornell University Press, 1977), 146.

22. Igor Levit, interview by Ari Shapiro, "Igor Levit: Tiny Desk Concert," November 22, 2019, https://www.npr.org/transcripts/781276601.

23. For discussion, see Richard I. Sugarman, *Levinas and the Torah: A Phenomenological Approach* (Albany, NY: SUNY Press, 2019).

24. For relevant discussion, see Esau McCaulley, *Reading While Black: African American Biblical Interpretation as an Exercise in Hope* (Downers Grove, IL: InterVarsity, 2020).

25. See Phyllis Trible's classic work, *Texts of Terror: Literary-Feminist Readings of Biblical Narratives* (Philadelphia: Fortress, 1984).

26. Wilda C. Gafney offers a spiritual discipline for such reading in *A Women's Lectionary for the Whole Church: A Multi-Gospel Single-Year Lectionary* (New York: Church Publishing, 2021). My thanks to Deanna Smith for pointing me to this resource.

27. Rita Felski, *Hooked: Art and Attachment* (Chicago: University of Chicago Press, 2020), 54–55, 75.

28. Felski, *Hooked*, 55, referring to Daniel Cavicchi, *Tramps like Us: Music and Meaning among Springsteen Fans* (Oxford: Oxford University Press, 1998).

29. Felski, *Hooked*, 58.

30. Marcel Proust, *Swann's Way*, trans. Lydia Davis (New York: Viking, 2002), 146.

31. Proust, *Swann's Way*, 146–47.

## Chapter 6: On Not Living Ahead of Time

1. David Hume, *Enquiries Concerning Human Understanding and Concerning the Principles of Morals*, 3rd ed., ed. P. H. Nidditch (Oxford: Clarendon, 1975), 18.

2. Hume, *Enquiries Concerning Human Understanding*, 18–19.

3. For a classic discussion of this vision, see Richard J. Mouw, *When the Kings Come Marching In: Isaiah and the New Jerusalem*, rev. ed. (Grand Rapids: Eerdmans, 2002).

4. Barry Lopez, *Arctic Dreams: Imagination and Desire in a Northern Landscape* (1986; repr., New York: Vintage, 2001), 75.

5. Lopez, *Arctic Dreams*, 75.

6. Augustine, Letter 189.5, in *Letters 156–210*, trans. Roland Teske, ed. Boniface Ramsey, *The Works of Saint Augustine* II/3 (Hyde Park, NY: New City, 2004), 261.

7. 2 Clement 6:3, 5–6, in *The Apostolic Fathers*, 3rd ed., ed. and trans. Michael W. Holmes (Grand Rapids: Baker Academic, 2007), 145.

8. Gustavo Gutiérrez, *A Theology of Liberation: History, Politics, Salvation*, rev. ed., trans. Sister Caridad Inda and John Eagleson (Maryknoll, NY: Orbis Books, 1988), 124.

9. Gutiérrez, *Theology of Liberation*, 115.

10. For more on this, see my discussion of "refugee spirituality" in *On the Road with Saint Augustine* (Grand Rapids: Brazos, 2019), 36–55.

11. Gutiérrez, *Theology of Liberation*, 132–33.

12. Edmund Husserl, *The Phenomenology of Internal Time-Consciousness*, trans. James S. Churchill (Bloomington: Indiana University Press, 2019), 23.

13. Husserl, *Phenomenology of Internal Time-Consciousness*, 95.

14. Heidegger, *Being and Time*, trans. John Macquarrie and Edward Robinson (San Francisco: Harper & Row, 1962), 329.

15. Heidegger, *Being and Time*, 373 (slightly modified to first person).

16. As Heidegger puts it, "Anticipatory resoluteness discloses the current Situation of the 'there' in such a way that existence, in taking action, is circumspectively concerned with what is factically ready-to-hand environmentally." Heidegger, *Being and Time*, 373. In other words, anticipation of the future to which I'm called discloses, illuminates, and reframes my present situation. But this only happens when I *act* toward the future.

17. Heidegger, *Being and Time*, 374.

18. Martin Heidegger, *The Phenomenology of Religious Life*, trans. Matthias Fritsch and Jennifer Anna Gosetti-Ferencei (Bloomington: Indiana University Press, 2004), 71–72 (slightly modified).

19. Heidegger, *Phenomenology of Religious Life*, 72.

20. Heidegger, *Phenomenology of Religious Life*, 73.

21. For a more in-depth exploration of these themes, see James K. A. Smith, *Awaiting the King: Reforming Public Theology* (Grand Rapids: Baker Academic, 2017).

22. Augustine, *The City of God* 10.17, trans. Henry Bettenson (New York: Penguin, 1984), 397–98.

23. Augustine, *City of God* 1.28 (trans. Bettenson, 39).

24. Augustine, *City of God* 5.preface (trans. Bettenson, 179).

25. Augustine, *City of God* 5.12 (trans. Bettenson, 196).

26. For Augustine, there can be true justice only where there is true worship. Since the pagan empire, as an outpost of the earthly city, could never be a site of true worship, it could never be home to true justice. However, that doesn't prevent Augustine from nonetheless affirming the goods of the empire which, *relatively speaking*, are preferable to anarchy. For discussion, see *City of God* 19.21–25 (trans. Bettenson, 881–91).

27. Jesse McCarthy, "Language and the Black Intellectual Tradition," in *Who Will Pay Reparations on My Soul?* (New York: Liveright, 2021), 151.

28. McCarthy, "Notes on Trap," in *Who Will Pay Reparations on My Soul?*, 131.

29. Martin Luther King Jr., "I Have a Dream," speech, August 28, 1963, Washington, DC, available at "Read Martin Luther King Jr.'s 'I Have a Dream' Speech in Its Entirety," NPR, updated January 14, 2022, https://www.npr.org/2010/01/18/122701268/i-have-a-dream-speech-in-its-entirety.

30. Oliver O'Donovan, *Desire of the Nations: Rediscovering the Roots of Political Theology* (Cambridge: Cambridge University Press, 1996), 151.

31. For more on this, see James K. A. Smith, "Faithful Compromise: The Lost Art of Brokered Effectiveness in Public Life," *Comment* (Spring 2014): 2–4.

32. O'Donovan, *Desire of the Nations*, 212.

33. For more detailed development of this theme, see Smith, *Awaiting the King*, 91–124.

34. Gutiérrez, *Theology of Liberation*, 125.

35. William Gibson, on NPR's *Fresh Air*, 1993, cited in Natasha Stagg, "Painting the End of the World," *Frieze*, April 20, 2021, https://www.frieze.com/article/natasha-stagg-chris-dorland.

36. As Terry Eagleton points out, "A professional or card-carrying optimist feels sanguine about specific situations because she tends to feel sanguine in general." *Hope without Optimism* (Charlottesville: University of Virginia Press, 2015), 1. He goes on to rightly point out that, whatever their professed political standpoint, "optimists are conservatives because their faith in a benign future is rooted in their trust in the essential soundness of the present" (4).

37. Eagleton, *Hope without Optimism*, 4.

38. Reinhold Niebuhr, *The Irony of American History* (1952), in *Reinhold Niebuhr: Major Works in Religion and Politics*, ed. Elisabeth Sifton (New York: Library of America, 2015), 510.

39. Cited in Winn Collier, *A Burning in My Bones: The Authorized Biography of Eugene H. Peterson* (Colorado Springs: WaterBrook, 2021), 149.

40. Calvin Seerveld, "Ordinary Aesthetic Life: Humor, Tastes and 'Taking a Break,'" in Calvin Seerveld, *Normative Aesthetics: Sundry Writings and Occasional Lectures*, ed. John H. Kok (Sioux Center, IA: Dordt College Press, 2014), 121.

41. Marilynne Robinson, *The Givenness of Things: Essays* (New York: Farrar, Straus & Giroux, 2015), 125.

**Epilogue**

1. Olivier Clément, *Transfiguring Time: Understanding Time in the Light of the Orthodox Tradition*, trans. Jeremy N. Ingpen (Hyde Park, NY: New City, 2019), 79.

2. Augustine, *Confessions* 9.3.6, trans. Henry Chadwick (Oxford: Oxford University Press, 1992), 159.